SENSELESS

Surviving Life's Tragedies

JERRY A. HICKSON

Warner Press
Anderson, Indiana

Coordinator of Publishing & Creative Services
Church of God Ministries, Inc.
PO Box 2420
Anderson, IN 46018-2420
800-848-2464 • www.chog.org

To purchase additional copies of this book, to inquire about distribution, and for all other sales-related matters, please contact:

Warner Press, Inc.
PO Box 2499
Anderson, IN 46018-2499
800-741-7721 • www.warnerpress.org

All Scripture quotations, unless otherwise indicated, are taken from the Holy Bible, New International Version®. NIV®. Copyright © 1973, 1978, 1984 by Biblica. Used by permission of Zondervan. All rights reserved.

Scripture quotations marked CEV are taken from the Contemporary English Version © 1991, 1992, 1995 by American Bible Society. Used by permission.

ISBN: 978-1-59317-630-3

Printed in the United States of America.

13 14 15 16 17 18 /CH/ 10 9 8 7 6 5 4 3 2 1

for Melissa

June 11, 1985–December 21, 1999

Contents

Section 1

Confronting Our Story

Chapter 1

Pushed to Your Limits?

All of us face hard times in life. We hope that if we do the right things, we will get a break, but we don't. We all suffer. Some of us experience horrific tragedy that is public knowledge, while others experience personal trials in secret. In either case, we wonder what to do when we are thrust into these harrowing, even hellacious experiences, despite our faithfulness to God.

Perhaps you have been injured by your own family. Home should be a safe place where people care deeply for you. But you may have grown up in a home where one or both parents inflicted abuse on you. Perhaps you married someone who hurt you deeply. Or perhaps your children have caused you pain. It is even more difficult to overcome the challenges of life when the people closest to us pose those challenges.

Perhaps your pain has come from your church family. Most churches encounter conflict, and some handle conflict better than others. We would like to think that God's house will be free of evil motives, shielded from destructive attitudes and behavior, but this is not true. Sometimes personal conflict results in a church split or in individuals being driven from the flock. You may be carrying scars from one or more painful experiences with church people.

Perhaps you lost a job and have gone for a protracted time without employment. In our Western culture, we derive much of our identity from the work we do. Applying for employment and being rejected is a blow to our self-esteem. A long period of unemployment has serious economic consequences that elevate anxiety and deepen depression. Changes in technology and culture can result in the permanent loss of job opportunities that we took for granted. The emotional result is no less painful than losing our job on account of incompetence or malfeasance.

Perhaps you have lost your home to fire or flood. How could you prepare for such a catastrophe? Due to events beyond your control, a lifetime of personal possessions and cherished memorabilia has been destroyed or permanently damaged. Insurance settlements may lessen the burden, but some things cannot be replaced. And you are left with the threat that something like this might happen again.

Perhaps a thief or embezzler has taken what you had. You feel betrayed or victimized by that person. Anyone who has experienced a home burglary will describe emotions similar to those of a rape victim. Your privacy was invaded. Someone took from you something they had no right to take.

Perhaps your physical person was indeed violated. Every day someone is raped or otherwise sexually assaulted. Many of these crimes are committed by someone within the family, someone the victim trusted. Many of these crimes are never reported, yet the victims feel broken and dirty.

Perhaps you are suffering a serious injury or illness. We all get sick or hurt from time to time, but some of us have acute physical problems that radically change our ability to function. Some of us have chronic diseases that restrict our daily activities. Not only has your body been damaged, but the malady eats away at your soul.

Perhaps someone you loved has died. Whether they were advanced in years or young, you are left without the company of a significant person in your life. You may have had warning as you watched them suffer a prolonged illness, or you may have been shocked to learn of their sudden passing—perhaps as the result of a tragic and unjust event or even suicide. In any case, you are now deprived of someone you loved.

Perhaps someone you love is suffering a debilitating disease such as Alzheimer's. Your grief is compounded by the fact that you continue to see the one you love, but they cannot remember you. You have watched them slide deeper and deeper into dementia, yet their body is healthy and they may continue to live for years. Perhaps this is your parent, your spouse, even your child. Every day the loss deepens, yet your loved one is still present.

Perhaps you have lost your spouse to divorce. It doesn't help to be told that divorce has become a common experience. You loved this person and thought you would spend your life with them, yet the relationship broke down. Now you are alone. You are troubled by the question, "Where did I fail?" Perhaps you have children who are now deprived of a parent or must shuttle between parents. Perhaps you have lost custody of your children. You may have done nothing wrong, but the divorce leaves you feeling like a moral and spiritual failure, stigmatized by your community.

Perhaps your parents have gotten divorced. This pain may be different for young children, teens, and adults, but we cannot deny that the pain is real and lasting. Perhaps your own ability to build a marital relationship with someone is hindered by the failure that was modeled before you. Family events that should be a cause of joy are complicated by the absence of a parent, or by the presence of both parents, accompanied by new spouses or significant others.

As I have shared with groups about these losses, I have encountered some whose pain is heightened by the fact that they suffer alone. We are built for relationship (Gen 2:18), yet many of us are single. Perhaps you have never married. Perhaps you are widowed or divorced. You are left without someone to walk with you as you endure life's hardships. This makes the times of trouble even more difficult.

Beyond all these personal calamities is our common hardship of a world gone mad. We are astounded at world events that are beyond our control. We see airliners deliberately steered into the World Trade Center towers, schoolyard shootings, wars in faraway lands, and natural disasters like tsunamis, earthquakes, and hurricanes.

These are examples of the tragedies of life. I am sure you can list others. We all experience them in one way or another, and you may feel you have had more than your fair share. How can you survive these rough passages? And how will they affect your relationship with God?

One of the purposes of the church is to help people deal with these challenges. The church should be a spiritual hospital where hurting souls can find healing. Unfortunately, Christians often make the problems worse with beliefs that seem biblical but are not and are destructive to faith. I have heard things said in conversation and preached in pulpits that rub salt in the wounds of sufferers and threaten to drive them away from the God who loves us and offers us healing. As I have served as a pastor and personally experienced some of the tragedies of life, I have developed four principles for surviving hard times. You will find that they contradict what people think is Christian teaching at some points, but hear me out.

Much of what I am sharing comes from my experience of having my first child born with multiple disabilities, which plunged us into struggles with medical, educational, and legal people until her tragic death at the age of fourteen.

Melissa is not my only experience with the tragedies of life, but may I tell you her story?

Chapter 2

Melissa's Story

Melissa was born on my twenty-eighth birthday, June 11, 1985. Elizabeth and I had been married for six years and had wanted a baby for three. A previous pregnancy had ended with a painful miscarriage. This pregnancy had not gone well, but we knew of no problems at the time of delivery. Within moments, Melissa began to make rasping noises with every breath, and doctors explained that the cartilage in her larynx was collapsing. The same lack of development was responsible for her ears being a little floppy. (Within days, this problem corrected itself.) From the first day, the doctors bombarded us with bad news about the health of our daughter.

They said there was something wrong with Melissa neurologically, but it would take us years to learn all the details. Melissa spent her first two weeks in the intensive care nursery, supplied with oxygen and hooked up to monitors to gauge her breathing and heartbeat. Every day after I returned from work, Elizabeth and I would spend the evening at Neo-Natology visiting our baby. While I was work, Elizabeth would catch a ride to the hospital to spend additional time with Melissa. Before taking Melissa home, we were required to receive training in CPR. The class was made up of my parents, Elizabeth, and me. I can still remember my business-executive father holding a doll on his knee and slapping her back, calling out, "Melissa. Melissa. Melissa." The memory seems grotesquely comical now, but there was nothing funny about it at the time.

After two weeks, we were permitted to take our baby home, but we were given an apnea monitor to make sure that she kept breathing through the night. We were staying with my parents at the time, as I was between jobs. For over a year, I had been searching for a church where I could serve; in the meantime, I worked at various temporary jobs in Dallas. We used a pair of bedrooms that were connected by a bathroom. During the night, the monitor would go off, causing us to bolt out of bed to check on Melissa. Every time, we would look at what we feared was a baby turning blue, only to find that she was fine and we would reset the alarm. And every time, in the doorway to the hall, would be the silhouette of two grandparents who were also awakened by the false alarm and who wanted to know if their granddaughter was all right without interfering with Melissa's parents.

Melissa had difficulty swallowing for the first month or so. She had a weak sucking reflex and would choke and turn blue. We had intended to breast feed our child, so Elizabeth had to use a breast pump. We would give Melissa the bottle as long as she could handle it. When she grew tired, we would switch to Gavache feeding. This means we poured the remainder of the milk down a tube that was almost always inserted in her nose. Part of the training we were given before taking Melissa home was the proper insertion of the feeding tube. We were to put a tube into a nostril and push it into her stomach. A large syringe would be attached to the end of the tube and we would listen with a stethoscope as air was forced through the tube. If we heard air rushing into the stomach, then Melissa was ready for feeding. If not, then the tube was in the lungs and had to be reinserted or Melissa would be drowned. (Even in the midst of such difficulties, we found moments of comic relief. My brother and his wife were having a second pregnancy a few months following Melissa's birth, so my nephew asked his mom if he could put the tube in when the baby came.)

Several times, Melissa had seizures in her crib. We gave her phenobarbital for a while until the seizures went away. Much later, Melissa would start having seizures again.

When Melissa was three months old, we moved to California, where I pastored a small church. We encountered an overwhelming variety of social workers from various agencies to help us with Melissa's various problems. Melissa missed most of the developmental mileposts. She was late in holding her head erect, crawling, walking, talking, and so on. Since Melissa was our first child, we were slow to notice these problems until informed by specialists. Melissa was inducted to the special education system at the age of three. Every morning, Melissa would board the bus with children at least twice her age.

The most notable visible indication of Melissa's problems was her facial paralysis. Melissa was a beautiful child with Moebius syndrome. Most of the nerves to her face never developed, so Melissa had no smile and was unable to blink her eyes or close her lips. She was unable to make the sounds "b," "p," "m," "r," "f," or "v." As Melissa grew, she developed interesting ways of substituting sounds. For "baby," she would say "gaygy." For "hamburger," she would say "hangurga." For "Mommy," she would say "nonny." So she might say, "Nonny gid hangurga to gaygy." Melissa would repeat herself once or twice to help you, and then would give up in disgust that you were so stupid.

One outcome of Melissa's facial paralysis was that her eyes were droopy, yet would not close. Melissa slept with her eyes open. Melissa learned that she could see better if she used her thumb to lift an eyelid. We had a surgery done to lift one of the eyelids slightly so that Melissa could see better. Melissa also had strabismus, a misalignment of the eyes. Many children are cross-eyed, Melissa was among the smaller group of children whose eyes wander out. This also was corrected by surgery. Unrelated to her eye problems, Melissa had a cleft palate. Fortunately, the cleft only went through the soft tissue in the back of the mouth and was easily corrected. This provided some help with swallowing and speech.

We had another child after going through extensive genetic testing to determine the risk of having another child like Melissa. As you can imagine, this was an anxious pregnancy. Danielle turned out to be healthy in that she had none of Melissa's issues. But when Danielle was three months old, we discovered that she had congenital glaucoma. She had to have four operations in a six-week period before this was corrected. Fortunately, the problem was discovered and corrected before any long-term damage occurred. Ironically, Danielle's glaucoma was discovered when she accompanied my wife to one of Melissa's eye exams. The normal routine was that one of us (usually Mom) would take a child to the doctor while the other (usually Dad) would babysit the other child at the office. On this day, I had an appointment, forcing Elizabeth to take both girls to the optometrist's office. It was a godsend that Danielle was at the doctor's office that day, where her problem was spotted by a professional.

During this time, we were making multiple trips to San Francisco (two hours away from Pacific Grove) for various doctor visits and hospitalizations for Melissa or Danielle. We wore out a Honda Civic making these trips. I purchased a used Isuzu when I decided I could no longer pray the old Honda back home reliably. We consumed more health insurance benefits than I can imagine. When Melissa was four years old, we moved to Florida to pastor a church there.

There we had our first experience with allegations of child abuse. We found that some in the public school system were more interested in protecting their workers than in protecting our child. We also discovered that the system could be a formidable opponent when we were accused of child abuse. We had to go through several investigations to be cleared. We retained attorneys, who suggested that we leave town before our child was permanently taken away from us, but we determined to stand our ground.

When Melissa was eight, we found that a surgery was available to help with her facial paralysis. We took her to a doctor in Virginia who could transplant a nerve from her hip to give her a smile. Part of the process was a series of tests where a needle was inserted in different places in Melissa's face and tongue to measure the presence of nerve activity. The tests confirmed the diagnosis that Melissa had no nerves in her face. This was so traumatic for Melissa that I had to get on the table and restrain her. We chose not to pursue this procedure as we no longer had health insurance and this doctor would not take Medicaid. We found another surgeon, who used a different procedure. He split the muscle used for chewing and sewed a thread to the corners of her mouth. By biting down, Melissa would be able to affect an artificial smile.

For years, I had prayed that Melissa would be able to smile. I believed that God could do this miraculously if he so chose. I was thrilled to find a surgical option that would allow Melissa to look more like other children. Melissa had to go a thousand miles to get the surgery done at Ohio State University. Dr. Anderson had pledged to provide the surgery at no expense. I advised the staff in advance that our daughter had a blood condition (polycythemia secondary) that made oxygenation and hydration difficult. I was met with patronizing responses as the staff treated me as a "worrisome father." On the day of the surgery, the anesthesiologist cancelled the operation when he found out about her blood condition. Consultations by a hematologist and a neurologist confirmed that her condition would complicate the surgery, but it could be done. We had to wait another week to get another slot in the operating room. It meant that I would be separated from my three girls for two weeks instead of one. I have never been as angry as I was that night. I took a long walk in the cold night air. Fortunately, the distance prevented me from acting in anger against those who ignored my warnings.

I had a vision in my mind of what Melissa would look like with a smile—it was a beautiful thing—but what I saw when Melissa came home was not what I had imagined. Her face was still wrapped in gauze, but I could see menacing stripes of green and black: the bruises from a traumatic procedure. Elizabeth told me this was a big improvement over what she looked like immediately after surgery. Elizabeth had taken pictures of Melissa right after the surgery. I looked at them once. I don't ever want to see them again. I stayed up all night, talking with my wife about the vision I had for Melissa and how painful the reality was for me. I have never wept like I did that night.

A new problem arose when Melissa was nine. It started with screams—full gut screams. She started doing this during a vacation as we traveled across the country. We first interpreted this as a behavioral issue and treated it as such. We took Melissa to neurologists and psychiatrists, who gave us no help. "These children act this way sometimes," was the counsel received from a psychiatrist for a fee of $150. I spent a full day working with Melissa trying to stop the screaming: the more I tried, the worse it got. On a vacation a year later, we took Amtrak across the country. Imagine having your child scream in marble-lined train stations and strangers looking to see who is abusing the child. We trained Melissa to cover her mouth when she screamed, which made no sense in light of what the psychiatrist said. If Melissa was doing this to get our goat, why did she comply with our requests to cover her mouth?

Finally, we found a developmental pediatrician who gave us a correct diagnosis. Dr. Frank Lopez was able to diagnose it over the phone before the first appointment. And he made arrangements to move our appointment up to the next morning. Melissa had a tic disorder: involuntary muscle activity. She was unable to have facial tics because of the Moebius syndrome. Most of her tics were verbal. She also had some arm and leg jerking. Tics are aggravated by stress, which explains why behavior modification methods were so counterproductive. With medication the screams were eliminated, but she would bark and grunt on occasion (when stressed by too much change). Melissa was fascinated with sound, so she would put words on her barks: "nicrogone," "docta." Sometimes she would hit or kick her sister or another child; it was difficult to diagnose whether she had done so intentionally or whether this was a tic. This was a strange disorder, and some well-intentioned Christians suggested that our daughter was demon-possessed.

I mentioned that Melissa had a blood disorder: this was called polycythemia. Melissa had too many red blood cells. Her blood was so thick and syrupy that she was at constant threat of a stroke-like event if the blood was unable to pass through a capillary. This issue played almost no role in Melissa's daily life: it was just a Damocles' sword hanging over her head. Perhaps such an event happened in the womb; we will never know. Two everyday symptoms of the condition were comedic. When she would go to the beach, her skin would turn beet red. More than once, we were chastised by strangers for taking our child to the beach without sunscreen when in fact she was wearing SPF 30. When she played in a cold mountain stream, her feet turned blue.

When Melissa was ten, I began to learn about civil rights for people like Melissa. We came to realize that the school system had taken several steps to deprive Melissa of her due. We began to advocate more aggressively to get Melissa a quality education.

When Melissa was twelve, we moved to Texas to plant a new church. We continued to work to get Melissa a decent education. The new school district had a strong reputation for understanding the needs of children like Melissa, so we began to think hopefully about what Melissa's adult life would be like. Would she ever be able to hold a job? Would she be able to live on her own?

Over the years, the seizures had returned. They usually happened in pairs, maybe two or four in a day, and her growth required an increase in the dosage of her seizure medication. She might go weeks or even months without a problem, but by the time Melissa turned fourteen, the seizures had increased to as many as twenty-four in a day. Melissa was admitted to an epilepsy center where the staff withdrew her medications and observed her with video cameras and monitors on her heart and brain. Melissa had two events in the first twenty-four hours. The doctors reported to us that these were not seizures but instances of cardiac arrest. We had grown accustomed to seizures, but this was a matter of life and death.

A surgeon gave Melissa a pacemaker to kick in when the heart tried to stop. Melissa had a good recovery from this surgery and was sent home. She spent a week in school, but on the Sunday before Thanksgiving 1999, Melissa became sick. It looked like the flu and a visit to the doctor produced that diagnosis. By Thanksgiving Day, Melissa's condition deteriorated to the point that we took her to the emergency room. Only there did we discover that she had a staph infection that had followed the pacemaker wire into her heart. Melissa was moved to a pediatric intensive care unit for IV antibiotic therapy.

That evening, Melissa slipped into a coma. Over the next month, the staph infection destroyed almost every organ in Melissa's body. Her blood pressure was only maintained with drugs injected through the IV tube. When Melissa's kidneys failed, she was given dialysis. On occasion, Melissa responded to family, but she never spoke nor got up from her bed after going to the hospital.

Several procedures were unsuccessful, and the lead doctor finally advised us that Melissa would not be able to recover. So we decided to discontinue life support. We gathered almost the entire family at the hospital. I was able to hold Melissa for an hour as the life ebbed out of her body. Then Melissa's mother held her for a while. Melissa died at 10:30 PM on Tuesday, December 21, 1999.

We had Melissa's funeral on the morning of Christmas Eve. Her funeral service was a celebration of joy and truth. The preacher declared that, like the little girl that Jesus found lying on her bed, Melissa had responded to the words *talitha cum*: "Little girl, get up." Is this not what we say we believe? Or are we just kidding ourselves to medicate our pain? I choose to take seriously the conviction that God has prepared for us a better place beyond death. Melissa will never again have a tic, seizure, or cardiac arrest. Melissa is able to speak her mind freely. And with her new body is a beautiful smile. So the marker on her grave carries only two words beyond her name and dates: "Smiling now."

Some have marveled at how well we handled Melissa's death. I suppose I could get angry with God if I believed he had done this terrible thing to us. But I knew that the all-powerful God was very present in this painful experience and cared deeply about Melissa and everyone in her family. In fact, the night that Melissa died was one of the most awesome experiences of my life. We all have to die sometime. I can think of no better way to go than to be surrounded by the family that loves you. And if I am to be angry about anything, it will not be the way Melissa died but the way she was born. I am still perplexed that Melissa entered life with so many things stacked against her. For me, that has been a far more difficult issue than her early deliverance to the better place that we expect awaits us. This book is an effort to explain how my wife and I survived the trauma of watching our child die, in the hope that others will be better able to bear their burdens by walking beside us.

We have had other tragedies in life, although they pale in comparison with the story of Melissa. Our house was badly damaged by water from a burst washing machine hose that spewed for days while we were away on a camping trip. The insurance settlement provided a wonderful upgrade for our house, but the process was painful, to say the least.

I had my driver's license taken from me twice because of an injury I incurred by falling from a ladder while painting my house. While the doctors testify that I am fully competent to drive, the legal process can be maddeningly slow. Twice, I have had to make special arrangements to get around while the state decided whether to reinstate my license.

While we were putting Danielle through college, my mother-in-law moved in with us as she experienced the effects of vascular dementia. My wife gave up her job to assume around-the-clock care of her mother, who was unable to understand her own limitations.

Shortly after my fiftieth birthday, I was informed that I had type-two diabetes and would have to radically change my lifestyle, relearning how to eat and taking exercise more seriously.

In June 2012, my car was totaled by a driver who failed to stop for a red light. Elizabeth witnessed the collision and surely would have been killed had she been riding with me.

I am sure you have stories of trial and suffering. Perhaps your stories make mine seem trivial. However, I believe we can survive the most trying experiences of life. I believe we can overcome all that life throws at us and live victoriously. In the following chapters, I want to share with you four principles to help you cope with life's troubles.

You may find help in reading this book alone, but I encourage you to study it with a group of people who have also been traumatized by life. I am confident that you can endure whatever has caused you pain and overcome every obstacle that still faces you. I pray that this book will be an aid to your journey.

Section 2

Four Principles

Chapter 3

Principle 1: God is still on his throne. Remember that.

Jason had served two terms in the National Guard. A year before his second term expired, his unit was activated to fight in Afghanistan. He left his young wife and newborn daughter to fulfill his duty. While his unit was repeatedly involved in combat with casualties, Jason was spared. When his term of duty was extended, his family endured the anxiety that many military families have experienced. Fortunately, Internet technology allowed them to remain in close contact with him. Finally, Jason's unit was brought back home. Jason was discharged from service and went back to work with the delivery company. While at work the first week, Jason was struck by an underage driver on a joy ride. After two days in intensive care, Jason died from the effects of internal bleeding and trauma. His family was overwhelmed with grief compounded by the senselessness of this death. After surviving months of harrowing combat, Jason's life was snuffed out by a random act of irresponsibility.

When life slaps us across the face and when it seems that all is chaos, we need to remember that there is a God and that he rules over all. God is still on his throne. This first principle is a point that is often preached, but when life gets stormy we are prone to forget it. Your life may seem out of control, but that does not disprove God's sovereignty. God rules the universe, even in your darkest hours.

If God's existence or power must be proved by our experience, then it is limited and contingent. Such an earthbound God would not deserve our worship.

We tend to think that because God is loving and all-powerful, then only good things happen to people who are faithful to him. This creates a problem when bad things happen to good people. We must conclude that (1) something is wrong with me, (2) God does not really love me, or (3) God is not all-powerful.

The Scriptures speak to this paradox between our faith in an all-powerful God and the reality that God allows his people to suffer:[1]

> Surely God is good to Israel,
>> to those who are pure in heart.
> But as for me, my feet had almost slipped;
>> I had nearly lost my foothold.
> For I envied the arrogant
>> when I saw the prosperity of the wicked.
> They have no struggles;
>> their bodies are healthy and strong.
> They are free from the burdens common to man;
>> they are not plagued by human ills.
> Therefore pride is their necklace;
>> they clothe themselves with violence.
> From their callous hearts comes iniquity;
>> the evil conceits of their minds know no limits.
> They scoff, and speak with malice;
>> in their arrogance they threaten oppression.

---

1. Other texts include Psalms 10:1 and Habakkuk 1:13.

Their mouths lay claim to heaven,
  and their tongues take possession of the earth.
Therefore their people turn to them
  and drink up waters in abundance.
They say, "How can God know?
  Does the Most High have knowledge?"
This is what the wicked are like—
  always carefree, they increase in wealth.
Surely in vain have I kept my heart pure;
  in vain have I washed my hands in innocence.
All day long I have been plagued;
  I have been punished every morning.
If I had said, "I will speak thus,"
  I would have betrayed your children.
When I tried to understand all this,
  it was oppressive to me
till I entered the sanctuary of God.
  (Ps 73:1–17)

Many have found their faith tested and even destroyed by the tragedies of life. When we are confused by the senselessness of our experience, we do well to enter the presence of God without preconceptions or conditions, as the psalmist did.

What do we mean when we say that God is "sovereign"? The president of the United States is sovereign over us, but we do not blame him for the potholes in our streets. We must be careful lest our imaginations extend the sovereignty of God to places that do not fit reality nor biblical teaching.[2] Popular theology has God pushing buttons to make everything happen. According to this view, everything that happens is part of the divine plan. On the

---

2. Brian McLaren offers a wonderful discussion of this perspective of sovereignty in contrast to mechanistic thinking (McLaren, *Secret Message of Jesus*, 52).

other hand, some believe that God is like a divine watchmaker who walks away from what he has made and has nothing more to do with it. Such a God refuses to get involved in the problems of the world he has created.

The God of the Bible is neither of these.

Classic Christian thinking holds that God is all-powerful (omnipotent) and perfect in his goodness (omni-benevolent). What implications can we draw from these convictions? How do we reconcile these truths with the tragedies of life?

Many Christians hold a simplistic (though thoroughly logical) belief that, since God is sovereign, all things happen at his directive. Kay Arthur writes, "All of history—including famines, droughts, plagues, and economic disasters—centers on what God wants to bring to pass regarding either Israel or the Church."[3] Later, she surmises, "Where is God when bad things happen? He's behind the curtains, directing, and overseeing it all."[4] Renowned for her faith in the wake of a paralyzing diving accident, Joni Eareckson Tada makes these statements, "Unless the Bible is wrong, nothing happens outside of God's decree," "No sin happens that he doesn't deliberately allow," and "No trial reaches us apart from God's explicit decree and specific permission."[5] In his book on theodicy, John Piper writes, "And what I mean in this chapter when I say that God is sovereign is not merely that God has the *power and right* to govern all things, but that he *does* govern all things, for his own wise and holy purposes."[6] Whether in books, magazine articles, sermons, or everyday conversation, many Christians assume that everything which happens to us is part of God's plan.

3. Arthur, *When Bad Things Happen*, 54.
4. Ibid., 129.
5. Tada, *When God Weeps*, 76, 222, 231.
6. Piper, *Suffering and the Sovereignty of God*, 19.

But is the truth that simple? Should we attribute everything that happens to us as a part of God's plan for us? Some fear that any other belief would deny the existence of God and reject the authority of the Bible. But many believers are able to balance the conviction that God is Lord over all things with the reality that things happen that make no sense. We will examine this further in the next chapter.

One misunderstanding arises from a translation of Romans 8:28. Some will quote, "All things work for good for those who love the Lord." This is based on the rendition given in the King James Version of 1611, but the most recent translations render this verse differently: "We know that in all things God works for the good of those who love him, who have been called according to his purpose" (Rom 8:28). The use of vocabulary here makes a big difference. Not all events have a good outcome; many produce an evil outcome. But God in his sovereignty is able to work through all things (including evil things) to bring benefits to his children. Based on the old (mis)translation of Romans 8:28, some insist that everything that happens is part of God's plan, yet many things that happen contradict what God has revealed about himself and his will for us. What happens in life is the result of many various causes, some of which are in direct conflict with the will of God. But no matter what happens by whatever cause, God strives to bless those who love him. That is what Romans 8:28 says, in awesome testimony to the persistent love of God, despite the fact that much of what happens in this world is irrational and troubling.

The question naturally arises, Why pray? If God allows us to suffer, what's the use of praying? Why ask God to intervene in our problems if we know that he won't? Some assert that prayer is more about getting us in line with God's will than it is about persuading God to change our circumstances. Yet the Bible clearly invites us to approach God in petition and intercession, and it indicates that our prayers do make a difference in how God acts in our world. On one hand, we cannot attribute everything that happens to God's will; on the other hand, we cannot conclude that God will never intervene in our lives. The classic Christian conviction is that God acts in history in response to our prayers. Therein lies our dilemma: How shall we recognize the unfairness of life and yet affirm the existence of a loving and all-powerful God who *sometimes* intervenes in our lives, in response to prayer?[7]

Classical theism is built on the pillar of an unchanging God. The philosophers use the word *immutability* to describe God and speak of Deity as "the Unmoved Mover." But the god of philosophy is not the God we find in the Bible.[8] The God of the Bible feels emotion for people:

> Hear, O heavens. Listen, O earth.
> For the Lord has spoken:
> "I reared children and brought them up,
> but they have rebelled against me.
> The ox knows his master,
> the donkey his owner's manger,
> but Israel does not know,
> my people do not understand."
> (Is 1:2–3)

> My people are determined to turn from me.
> Even if they call to the Most High,
> he will by no means exalt them.

---

7. Since an extended conversation on prayer is beyond the scope of this book, I encourage you to read one of these: Yancey, *Prayer*; Foster, *Prayer*; Nouwen, *Way of the Heart*.

8. Richard Vieth offers a wonderful discussion on the implications of immutability (Vieth, *Holy Power, Human Pain*, 86–109). Stoicism must be corrected by pathos. He shows how classic Christology is incompatible with immutability. Further, an immutable God cannot enter into an authentic relationship with us. He discussed the contributions made by Whitehead's process theology, Heschel's God of the prophets, and Moultmann's theology of the cross.

How can I give you up, Ephraim?
    How can I hand you over, Israel?
How can I treat you like Admah?
    How can I make you like Zeboiim?
My heart is changed within me;
    all my compassion is aroused.
I will not carry out my fierce anger,
    nor will I turn and devastate Ephraim.
For I am God, and not man—
    the Holy One among you.
    I will not come in wrath.
    (Hos 11:7–9)

Philosophers imagine a god who feels nothing and never changes his mind. The Bible testifies of a loving God whose compassion is real. Schilling says, "Perennially, God does descend into the depths of our hells, whether we dig them ourselves or are thrust into them. But he is there with us, and in the consciousness we can find with him the way of healing."[9] In the midst of your struggle, remember that there is a God who cares about you. We will explore this further in chapter five.

When I was teaching this principle at one church, the class leader made a profoundly wise statement. He said, "If we know Jesus, this life is as bad as it gets. If we do not know Jesus, this life is as good as it gets."[10]

We do not need to deceive ourselves into believing that everything is wonderful. Some things about life are difficult and painful. But we can take solace in the assurance that God is on his throne. If we will hold out a little longer, things will get better. Before we envy those who are not faithful to God, let

---

9. Schilling, *God and Human Anguish*, 248–58.
10. Steve Pierce, Tigard Church of God

us remember their destiny. As painful as life can sometimes be, we can hold onto God's promises because we know he will keep them in the end.

There are many conflicting ideas about the implications of God's sovereignty, but Christians agree that we have a loving and all-powerful God who remains on the throne, no matter how rough life becomes. This still does not explain why bad things happen, but it is the basis of our hope. Whatever happens to us, we can be sure that God will be our Companion throughout our journey and bring good out of every evil.

An increasing number of people are not convinced that God exists. Trust me, when you are being pummeled by life, your experience of those troubles depends wholly on whether or not you understand that there is a God. If there is no God, then life truly is dismal and suicide might make sense. In the months following Melissa's birth, Elizabeth and I befriended a young couple whose child was severely damaged during a home birth in which the umbilical cord strangled the baby during delivery. This couple did not share our Christian background. They loved their baby as much as we loved ours, but they did not believe in God. Their absence of hope was in stark contrast to our confidence in the love of God, made available to us by our heritage of faith.

God's existence is not invalidated by the hardships we face. As much as the atheist touts the problem of evil as proof that there is no God, the existence of good is just as problematic.[11] As the sixth-century philosopher Boethius said, "If God is, whence come evil things? If he is not, whence come good?"[12] In either case, we are faced with perplexity.

---

11. Schilling, *God and Human Anguish*, 37. Materialism is often defined as an obsession with gaining possessions. The definition used here is that materialism is the belief that nothing exists that is not tangible, thus there is no God.

12. Boethius, *Consolation of Philosophy*, Book 1, 16.

Ethicist Lewis Smedes reflected on the terrorist attacks of September 11, 2001, and came to this conclusion:

> I have given up asking why such bad things happen. Instead, I look to the future and ask, When is God going to come and purge evil from God's world? When will God come to make God's original dream for the world come true?
>
> For me, there was no mystery about where God was and what God was up to on the morning of September 11, 2001. God was right there doing what God always does in the presence of evil that is willed by humans—fighting it, resisting it, battling it, trying God's best to keep it from happening. This time evil won. God, we hope, will one day emerge triumphant over evil—though, on the way to that glad day, God sometimes takes a beating.[13]

I am sure that God understands when we are confused, when life is spinning out of control and it seems there couldn't possibly be a God. Even when it seems that evil has won the upper hand, God is on his throne. This never-changing truth provides a solid rock on which we can stand when the waves are crashing in around us.

There are other issues to consider and questions to answer. But if you are in the middle of the maelstrom, remember this: God is, even when you cannot see any evidence of God.

---

13. Smedes, "What's God Up To?, 38–39.

Questions for Discussion

1. What kind of experiences challenge your confidence that God is sovereign?

2. What difference does it make to you in these experiences to know that God is sovereign?

3. What difference would it make if you knew the atheist was correct?

4. Why do you suppose so many people go from a belief in the sovereignty of God to the idea that everything is planned by God? Discuss the meaning of Romans 8:28.

Chapter 4

Principle 2:
Life is not fair.
Embrace it.

Crystal followed the Lord faithfully from the age of ten. She lived a life of purity in a sex-crazed world until she met the man of her dreams while on a mission trip to Rwanda. While delivering their first child, Crystal suffered a miscarriage and complications that led to her painful death. Living in the next apartment was a man known as Blade, a drug user with a history of involvement in a racist gang. In contrast to Crystal and her grieving husband, Blade had fathered several illegitimate children and lived in apparent prosperity.

Samuel Granillo was a junior at Colorado's Columbine High School when Eric Harris and Dylan Klebold killed twelve students and a teacher in April 1999. In July 2012, Granillo was in the Century Theater in Aurora, Colorado, when James Holmes killed twelve and wounded fifty-eight others. In the aftermath, Granillo told reporters, "Life is just not fair."

We like to entertain the notion that life somehow makes sense, but our daily news reports clearly demonstrate that it doesn't. Hear the cry of the prophet Habakkuk, who was disturbed by the plight of the people of Israel as they suffered exile:

How long, O Lord, must I call for help,
    but you do not listen?
Or cry out to you, "Violence!"
    but you do not save?
Why do you make me look at injustice?
    Why do you tolerate wrong?
Destruction and violence are before me;
    there is strife, and conflict abounds.
Therefore the law is paralyzed,
    and justice never prevails.
The wicked hem in the righteous,
    so that justice is perverted.
    (Hab 1:2–4)

Jeremiah is another prophet who experienced the downfall of the kingdom of God's people. His complaint echoes in the mind of every believer who faces the tragedies of life.

You are always righteous, O LORD,
    when I bring a case before you.
Yet I would speak with you about your justice:
    Why does the way of the wicked prosper?
    Why do all the faithless live at ease?
You have planted them, and they have taken root;
    they grow and bear fruit.
You are always on their lips
    but far from their hearts.
Yet you know me, O LORD;
    you see me and test my thoughts about you.
Drag them off like sheep to be butchered.
    Set them apart for the day of slaughter.
How long will the land lie parched
    and the grass in every field be withered?

Because those who live in it are wicked,
   the animals and birds have perished.
Moreover, the people are saying,
   "He will not see what happens to us."
   (Jer 12:1–4)

The followers of Jesus confronted this dilemma when they encountered a man born blind (John 9:1–3). They wanted to know if his disability was the consequence of his own sin or something he inherited. Jesus responded that truth does not fit into this simple equation. On another occasion, Jesus was informed of a current events story involving a horrible massacre (Luke 13:1–5). Jesus used this tragedy to launch into a discussion of sin and suffering. He reminded them of the collapse of a tower leading to the death of eighteen people. While this passage is puzzling, Jesus seems to be implying that there is no direct correlation between righteous living and prosperity or between sinful life and suffering. Life is not fair.

Certainly, other verses indicate that God is good to those who obey him while living in sin results in God's punishment. This is known as the Deuteronomic formula. A classic statement of this concept is found in Psalm 1.

Blessed is the man
   who does not walk in the counsel of the wicked
or stand in the way of sinners
   or sit in the seat of mockers.
But his delight is in the law of the Lord,
   and on his law he meditates day and night.
He is like a tree planted by streams of water,
   which yields its fruit in season
and whose leaf does not wither.
   Whatever he does prospers.

Not so the wicked.
> They are like chaff
> that the wind blows away.
Therefore the wicked will not stand in the judgment,
> nor sinners in the assembly of the righteous.
For the Lord watches over the way of the righteous,
> but the way of the wicked will perish.
> (Ps 1:1–6)

Clearly, this is poetry engaging in hyperbole. The reader who insists on interpreting this as a cardinal axiom of God's dealing with humanity must reconcile it with other parts of the Bible and with our own experience of the realities of life. While God is good to those who obey him, this does not guarantee that justice always prevails. Life is not fair.

We want to extend the sovereignty of God to a point that everything in our lives is part of God's purpose. A common statement is, "There must be a reason..." During his first inaugural speech, George W. Bush said, "I believe that things happen for a reason." This sound bite was included in a song played repeatedly on Christian radio stations.[1]

This concept expresses itself in various ways. Many times, a well-meaning person would try to comfort me with, "God must have known that you were strong enough to handle a child like Melissa." Do you think that made me feel any better? Such counsel prompted me to think I would rather that God had given *you* a child like Melissa so that I could have a healthy child.

The theology that God ordains everything that happens is not healthy, because we end up blaming God for our pain. This is completely backwards. We are tempted to tell someone who is suffering that life is just in the long run, though we may not see

---

1. Russ Lee, "Live What I Believe," Sparrow Records, 2002.

the scales of justice balanced at the moment. But this implies there is always a reason for suffering, so the sufferer must conclude that God allowed or inflicted suffering upon them. We are not helping our friends with such counsel. We are pushing them away from God. If they follow through to the logical end of such a rationale, they are likely to respond to God in anger. And we will have provoked that response.

This brings us to the question of theodicy. Theodicy is a part of philosophical and theological thought. The key question of theodicy is, Why does a loving (or good) and all-powerful God allow suffering? Theodicy is a more complex topic than we can fully address here.[2] For the sake of simplicity, we might diagram the problem with a triangle:

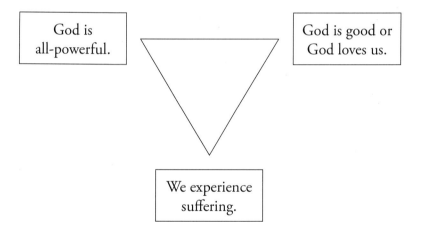

It seems impossible to reconcile these three ideas, which might be called the Great Triadox.[3] People have proposed several ways to explain it. Among the alternatives are:

---

2. For a more detailed discussion of theodicy, see chapter seven. Other books are referenced there that go more deeply than the scope of this book.

3. Others convert the word *dilemma* to *trilemma*.

- God can do something about evil but doesn't care.

- God cares, but cannot do anything about our pain.

- Evil is not real.

None of these solutions are acceptable to the Christian.[4] The first describes a being that is not the loving God portrayed in the Bible. The second describes a being that is not a god at all. The third is patently absurd to anyone who's experiencing evil, but it is the solution offered by Mary Baker Eddy, the founder of Christian Science, who said that evil and pain are illusory.[5]

People approach the problem of theodicy from a variety of perspectives. While some speak of the sovereignty of God, most speak of omnipotence and whether God can do anything about the problem. Some speak more of the goodness of God than about whether or not he loves us. Some speak of this as the problem of suffering, others as the problem of pain, and still others as the problem of evil. While there are certainly shades of difference in the meanings of these words, I tend to use them interchangeably.

An early Christian theologian suggested an ingenious way to balance all three points of the triangle. This solution was offered by Augustine (d. 430), who as a young man followed a dualistic religion that categorized all things as either evil or good. As a Christian, Augustine rejected this idea and pointed out that evil has no existence of its own.

Evil is not a created thing, Augustine insisted. Rather, evil is the absence of good. This can be illustrated in at least three ways. How do we make darkness? Only by extinguishing the light. Likewise, we do not create cold; refrigeration is simply the process

---

4. An excellent discussion of responses to the Great Triadox is found in Vieth, *Holy Power, Human Pain*, 17–58.

5. Mary Baker Eddy was the founder of Christian Science. The group is commonly considered a cult. I would suggest these teachings are neither Christian nor science.

of removing heat from a system. The creation account does not identify a day on which God created silence, because silence is not something created, but rather the state that exists when there is no sound. Darkness does not exist; it is the absence of light. Cold does not exist; it is the absence of heat. Likewise, silence is nothing more than the absence of sound. So Augustine concluded that we do not need to explain how God created evil, because evil does not exist. Evil is simply the absence of good. Everything God created is good.

God gave us the power of moral choice, the freedom to decide for ourselves how we will live. This means that we have the option of making wrong choices. However, moral choice is the greatest gift God could have granted us. God certainly had the ability to make things work differently, but consider the alternative: Pain and death are the result of sin, and sin is an option presented by moral choice. So the only way to avoid the quagmire of sin, pain, and death would have been for God to withhold from us the power of moral choice. Being all wise, God has created our world as a place of moral choice.

Certainly, some of the pain we experience is the consequence of choices we have made. When I present this in class, I draw a pie chart with a small sliver of a slice that represents the part of our suffering that we deserve because of choices we have made ourselves. One of my students insisted that his portion of the blame was a little larger. Indeed, there is a price to pay for our foolish actions, and we have all suffered such consequences. But more often, pain is the consequence of living in a fallen world. It is not "all part of the plan," it is "all part of the planet." So long as we live in this world, we share in its suffering, regardless of how we live our lives.

When we suffer, it's easy to torment ourselves with the thought that "God must be punishing me" because all of us have made enough sinful choices to make this seem plausible. Is there anyone who has never sinned? The Bible clearly says there is not.[6] Of course, if we think this through, we come to realize that other people have sinned more and suffered less. On the other hand, our world has plenty of people whose suffering is undeserved. Remember, life is not fair. So it's a mistake to link sin and suffering as cause and effect.

Even with a moral-choice theodicy, we are hard-put to explain natural disasters.[7] Do such things happen because we humans have damaged God's perfect creation? Some passages of the Bible support such a thought,[8] but the logic doesn't hold together. On one hand, it's fairly easy to argue that human sin is responsible when a drunk driver runs over a child. But what have humans done to God's creation to cause earthquakes, floods, tornadoes, and volcanoes? God does not ordain these destructive events, so is the earth itself permanently damaged by sin? It may be that most natural disasters are not the result of divine will or human decision, but simply creation unfolding apart from divine directive.[9]

Many have found solace in Leslie Weatherhead's discussion of God's Intentional Will, Circumstantial (or permissive) Will, and Ultimate Will. The key is remembering that nothing evil is of God's intention. God's Intentional Will may not be done because God must adapt to decisions made by others. Even in that case, God's will proves victorious in the end, no matter what challenges are presented by the wills of others.[10]

Much that is wrong has no reason. We want so badly for everything to have a reason, for things to make sense.[11] But the

---

6. 1 Kings 8:46; Psalms 53:3; Proverbs 20:9; Romans 3:23; 1 John 1:8.

7. Stackhouse extends natural evil to the "dog eat dog" reality of most of creation. What does the struggle for survival say about God? (Stackhouse, *Can God Be Trusted?*, 34–36).

8. Genesis 3:17-18; Romans 8:18-25.

9. I will discuss this further in chapter 9.

10. Weatherhead, *Will of God*.

11. In *Man's Search for Meaning*, Frankl showed that when we encounter a meaningless situation, we are compelled to imagine a meaning.

reality is, much in life is unjust and God's intentions may be temporarily thwarted. The Bible clearly teaches that what God does is always good and God is not the source of evil.

> When tempted, no one should say, "God is tempting me." For God cannot be tempted by evil, nor does he tempt anyone…. Every good and perfect gift is from above, coming down from the Father of the heavenly lights, who does not change like shifting shadows. (James 1:13, 17)

Whatever cause we may blame for suffering, we must not blame God. God loves us and offers healing when we suffer. As much as we would like to believe that everything makes sense and every story will have a happy ending, injustice is the reality of our world. We need to accept that fact.

We have a choice to make: We can accept the painful reality of the world in which we live, or we can delude ourselves with ideas that seem to be in keeping with biblical teaching but are not. We may not like some things that life brings our way, and we are certainly entitled to resist injustice. But if God intended everything that happens to us, we would have every right to be fatalists. Life often seems to contradict Scripture's message that God is good, but that doesn't disprove the Bible; it proves that life sometimes defies God. This does not lessen the pain of our loss and suffering, but it might spare us from holding unrealistic expectations about God. The best way to overcome the pain of loss is to embrace it fully, not repress it.[12]

Consider this: Christ dying for us on the cross was certainly not fair.[13] The core of the gospel message is that Jesus gave himself as the ultimate statement of love, and for that he was crucified.

---

12. See chapter 13, "Embracing the Pain," for more on this.
13. Wiersbe, *Why Us?*, 75–87. In chapter 6 ("The God Who Cares"), Wiersbe discusses the reality of God's love and the way it intersects with our experience of suffering.

No one has experienced pain like God did in watching his Son die. We can take this point one step further. Christians assert that Jesus was God in flesh; so God not only watched his Son die, God himself experienced death as an act of love for us. If we believe that life is fair, we ignore the reality of the cross.

The cross is the ultimate answer to the question of theodicy. God does care about our suffering, and God has done something about it. God has joined us in our suffering.[14]

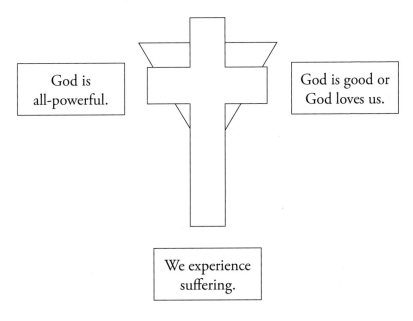

God is
all-powerful.

God is good or
God loves us.

We experience
suffering.

14. We will get back to the idea of the cross as evidence of God's care for us in the next chapter.

Questions for Discussion

1. Do you believe there is a reason for everything that happens to you?

2. How do you deal with scriptures that suggest God controls everything that happens?

3. What are the alternatives to a moral-choice theodicy?

4. How does acceptance of the injustice of life help us cope with adversity and loss?

5. Why do you suppose God intervenes at some times and not others?

Chapter 5

Principle 3:
There are persons who care about you.
Lean on them.

You are not alone. You have family and friends who want to help you through your challenges. The Bible says, "God sets the lonely in families" (Ps 68:6). Above all, God is available to you as "an ever-present help in trouble" (Ps 46:1). This is the flip side to principle one. The reason that we began with the sovereignty of God is that this offers us a foundation on which we can stand when life comes crashing down around us.

There is a tendency when facing tough times to draw into a shell. We feel battered by disappointments. The next step is to imagine that no one cares and that we are truly alone. Life is difficult enough without compounding the issues with isolation and self-pity. The harder things get, the more you need to draw near to family and friends.

No matter how difficult life may be, God is present at all times as a rock, a bulwark, a mighty fortress.[1] As the Bible says, "The name of the Lord is a strong tower; the righteous run to it and are safe" (Prov 18:10). With the psalmist, we can say, "Whom have I in heaven but you? And earth has nothing I desire besides

---

1. Weirsbe offers a helpful chapter titled "You Never Suffer Alone" (Wiersbe, *Why Us?*).

you. My flesh and my heart may fail, but God is the strength of my heart and my portion forever" (Ps 73:25–26).

At times, leaning on God includes raging with him.[2] Some people are surprised at this suggestion. Many books that address the topic of suffering go to great lengths to defend God. The argument is that we must submit to God in all things. It seems that screaming at God is the last thing a Christian should do. God has big shoulders and can handle your complaints. The Psalms are full of laments in which people complain to God, sometimes in bitter terms. The great Abraham dared to argue with God. Much of the book of Job is an account of the righteous man raging at God. Moses was so upset with God that he dared God to take his life. Raging at God is the action of a believer who feels wronged. One who does not believe in God ignores God completely. As expressed by Stanley Hauerwas, "Ironically, the act of unbelief turns out to be committed by those who refuse to address God in their pain, thinking that God just might not be up to such confrontation."[3]

How is your relationship with God? People who have nurtured their relationship with God are able to work through the rage to find comfort and support in the Paraclete.[4] Conversation with a total stranger is not easy. We benefit from investing time and effort in getting to know God before the storm clouds gather. When one is well acquainted with God, one is equipped to confront whatever emotions come when facing the tragedies of life. Then one can receive comfort from God to sustain until the clouds break.

The tragedies of life will cause us to wonder if God cares. The gospel answers that question. The cross is the ultimate statement of God's position in the face of evil. God does care. God has done something.

---

2. John K. Roth provides an example of raging at God in "A Theology of Protest," providing a process theology approach to theodicy (7–22).

3. Hauerwas, *Naming the Silences*, 84.

4. A name for the Holy Spirit that focuses on the roles of intercession and advocacy.

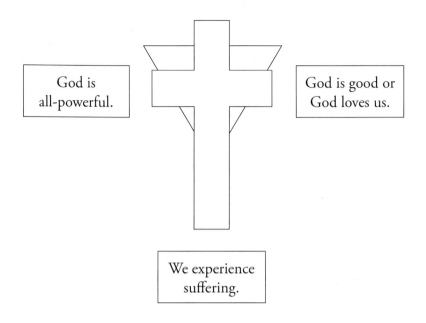

This is another place where classic Christian doctrine has done us a disservice. In affirming that God never changes, we deny an aspect of the personhood of God. The immutable and impassible god of the philosopher who never experiences emotion is not the God of Abraham, Isaac, and Jacob. The God of the Bible repents of creating people. "The LORD was grieved that he had made men on earth, and his heart was filled with pain" (Gen 6:6).[5] God displays his own suffering repeatedly through the prophetic witness (as in Hosea 11). To use the parental analogy again, God says, "This is hurting me more than it hurts you." (I hesitate to use this analogy as it usually comes in connection with disciplinary action, and I am not prepared to equate all suffering with punishment for wrongdoing.) Our God is a God of infinite compassion.

Perhaps there is some solace in the perception that we are not the only ones pained by our hardships: God loves us and

---

5. See also 1 Samuel 15:11, where God repents of choosing Saul as king.

participates in our suffering. By becoming one of us, Jesus has joined us in our suffering. German theologian Jürgen Moltmann puts it this way: "When God becomes man in Jesus of Nazareth, he not only enters into the finitude of man, but in his death on the cross also enters into the situation of man's godforsakenness."[6] When we are in our darkest moments, we can find commonality in the passion of Jesus.

> The crucified God is near to him in the forsakenness of every man. There is no loneliness and no rejection which he has not taken to himself and assumed in the cross of Jesus. There is no need for any attempts at justification or for any self-destructive self-accusations to draw near to him. The godforsaken and rejected man can accept himself where he comes to know the crucified God who is with him and has already accepted him. If God has taken upon himself death on the cross, he has also taken upon himself all of life and real life, as it stands under death, law, and guilt. In doing so he makes it possible to accept life whole and entire and death whole and entire.[7]

As the old spiritual says, "Nobody knows the trouble I've seen. Nobody knows but Jesus." The cross provides testimony that God knows and understands our dilemma.[8]

The apostle Paul exults in the message of the cross and what this means for facing the tragedies of life. Instead of complaining about his sufferings, Paul views these as an opportunity to join Christ in what he experienced:

---

6. Moltmann, *Crucified God*, 276.

7. Ibid., 277.

8. Peter Kreeft offers a wonderful discussion of this in his seventh chapter: "The Clues Converge: Jesus, the Tears of God" (Kreeft, *Making Sense Out of Suffering*, 129–40). Jeffry Zurheide discusses Barth's interpretation of the cross in *When Faith Is Tested: Pastoral Responses to Suffering and Tragic Death* (35–48).

I want to know Christ and the power of his resurrection and the fellowship of sharing in his sufferings, becoming like him in his death. (Phil 3:10)

I consider that our present sufferings are not worth comparing with the glory that will be revealed in us. The creation waits in eager expectation for the sons of God to be revealed. For the creation was subjected to frustration, not by its own choice, but by the will of the one who subjected it, in hope that the creation itself will be liberated from its bondage to decay and brought into the glorious freedom of the children of God.

We know that the whole creation has been groaning as in the pains of childbirth right up to the present time. Not only so, but we ourselves, who have the firstfruits of the Spirit, groan inwardly as we wait eagerly for our adoption as sons, the redemption of our bodies. For in this hope we were saved. But hope that is seen is no hope at all. Who hopes for what he already has? But if we hope for what we do not yet have, we wait for it patiently.

In the same way, the Spirit helps us in our weakness. We do not know what we ought to pray for, but the Spirit himself intercedes for us with groans that words cannot express. And he who searches our hearts knows the mind of the Spirit, because the Spirit intercedes for the saints in accordance with God's will. (Rom 8:18–27)

Like Paul, we must develop a theology of suffering. That theology must take into consideration that Jesus also suffered. In so doing, Christ joins us in our suffering. We are not alone.

God has also provided our family and close friends as means of support. At the beginning of the Bible, God says, "It is not good for the man to be alone" (Gen 2:18). There is no worse time to be alone than when battered by the tragedies of life. We need to reach out for support from our family and the people who love us. Gerald Sittser knows what it is to survive the tragedies of life, having experienced a collision that killed his four-year-old daughter, his wife, and his mother. Sittser says, "Not only must people who want to comfort someone in pain make a decision to do so, but people who need the comfort must also decide to receive it. Their responsibility will include facing the darkness with courage, learning new skills, and striving for mutuality in friendships."[9] You cannot afford to pull into a shell. You must lean on those who care about you.

Leslie Weatherhead suggests that by seeking the counsel of others, we can better discern the will of God in difficult times. We might be helped by seeking the advice of a wise Christian friend or a group of friends at church.[10]

When everything comes crashing in on us, we must realize that we are not alone. Many have been helped in facing the tragedies of life by the well-known poem "Footprints."[11] When we cannot even walk, we have One who walks with us and for us. We have others we can lean on when we cannot stand. And we need to consider that this point goes both ways. We need to recognize that there are people all around us who are in need of our support.

I love to collect proverbs. The Bible offers a whole book of proverbs.[12] There are more proverbs to be found throughout the rest of the Bible. A proverb offers a nugget of wisdom in a few words. My favorite one says, "Everyone is bleeding on the inside and trying not to let it show." If you are not hurting right now, look at the person next to you: they probably are in pain, even though you see no evidence of it.

---

9. Sittser, *Grace Disguised*, 162–63.
10. Weatherhead, *Will of God*, 65–69.
11. By Mary Stephenson.
12. I count 592 proverbs in the book of Proverbs, mostly one-verse couplets.

When trying to console a hurting person, they may well make statements such as, "It is God's will," or may ask for an explanation of why God would do this to them. Rather than try to correct their theology, allow them to express their grief. Their false belief of determinism can be confronted later if it is doing more harm than good.[13] Each Christian is responsible for sharing the love of God with those who are suffering the tragedies of life. My final chapter offers some guidelines on ministering effectively to such people.

We were able to survive the birth, life, and death of Melissa because we had people who cared about us. When Melissa was born, we had the good fortune to be living at my parents' home. (Yes, I said "good fortune." While living with parents would normally be considered a handicap for a young married couple, their home turned out to be a wonderful shelter in our time of suffering.) Over the years, we had supportive congregations and friends. Melissa always had people who loved her because of her unique challenges. At all times, God was faithful.

As God said through the prophet: "When you pass through the waters, I will be with you; and when you pass through the rivers, they will not sweep over you. When you walk through the fire, you will not be burned; the flames will not set you ablaze. For I am the LORD, your God" (Is 43:2–3a). Are you having trouble believing that God cares about you? Listen to this. "God has said, 'Never will I leave you; never will I forsake you.' So we say with confidence, 'The Lord is my helper; I will not be afraid'" (Heb 13:5b–6a). "Do not fear, for I am with you; do not be dismayed, for I am your God. I will strengthen you and help you; I will uphold you with my righteous right hand" (Is 41:10).[14]

---

13. Zurheide, *When Faith Is Tested*, 20. Surin concludes that theodicy as a mental exercise is useless except that it leads to action to ease the pain of the person who suffers (Surin, *Theology and the Problem of Evil*, 162). See also Vieth, *Holy Power, Human Pain*, 118–19, and Stackhouse, *Can God be Trusted?*, 67.

14. Other scriptures of encouragement include Psalm 27:5; 28:7; 71:3; 73:25–26; Proverbs 14:26; 18:10; Isaiah 25:4.

There really are persons who care about you. Whether you believe it or not, God loves you and cares deeply about your suffering. There are surely others around you who will help you get through this. Give them a chance to share God's love with you. While you are at it, you might find someone who needs to lean on you. It is amazing how bearing the load of another makes our own a little lighter. Life is enough of a challenge without compounding your load with self-pity. Call out to God and find others on whom you can lean through the times of hardship. And allow others to lean on you.

Questions for Discussion

1. What resources have you found in friends and family that have helped you through the tragedies of life?

2. How has God been a help to you in coping with the tragedies of life?

3. Do you sometimes find yourself raging at God?

4. How does the cross provide comfort in times of trial?

5. How can we help others cope with life?

6. How is unconditional love a resource for coping with life?

Chapter 6

Principle 4:

You are solely responsible for the choices you make today.

Do something.

There is not much you can do about most of your circumstances, but you can always choose your response to your circumstances. There is a time for reflection, when we ruminate on what has gone wrong; but then we must get up and carry on with life. No one can do this for you. You must decide what you will do with the wrongs and injustices that life has dealt you.

Jesus came upon a man who was lying beside a pool waiting for help. He had been unable to walk for thirty-eight years. When Jesus encountered him, he asked an insightful question: "Do you want to get well?" (John 5:6c). The man responded with excuses about how things never worked out right, how no one would help him get into the water when the moment was right. Jesus looked into his eyes and said, "Get up." The man had to take Jesus at his word and take action for himself. Or he could stay by that pool for another thirty-eight years. So how about it: Do you want to get well?

The book of Job offers some wonderful guidance on acting in response to suffering. Many mistakenly think that Job addresses the question of theodicy. The book of Job was not written to solve the problem of theodicy; it is a discussion of how God's people respond to suffering.[1] Notice that God never answers Job's question. For thirty-six chapters Job questions God. God never gives Job any answers. In fact, when God does show up, he only questions Job. But Job responds to his suffering as a righteous person. Job's wife offers a contrast in character, saying, "Are you still holding on to your integrity? Curse God and die" (Job 2:9). In the midst of all his questions, Job makes a statement of powerful faith, "I know that my Redeemer lives, and that in the end he will stand upon the earth" (Job 19:25). No one but Job could decide how he would respond to the terrible things that happened to him. And you alone determine your course out of this current dilemma.

All too often, we want to project the blame on others—on God, on people, on things. We must take ownership of our decisions. We can't remake the past, but we have control over our future. Everything hinges on what we do in the present. In every circumstance, we must choose how we will respond to God. You must decide what you believe about life and about God. You must decide how to put the pieces together to play the hand that you have been dealt.

This is another aspect of the discussion we have been having about free will. If God decides everything, then we can just shrug our shoulders, blame God, and give up. But life is not that simple. There are many things in life that are not fair, that make no sense, that are beyond our control. We are responsible for our choices. You may not be responsible for getting yourself into this mess, but you are responsible for what you do now. No one but you can decide what you will do next. God himself is waiting to see what you will do and is eager to help you along the way.

---

1. In chapter 11, I discuss Job at length.

The great ethicist, H. Richard Niebuhr suggests that the core concept is responsibility: how shall we to respond to what has happened to us? We could easily fall into the trap of determinism, to see what has happened as God's will. Neibuhr rejects such simplistic thinking.[2] Without blaming God for everything that has happened to us, we must determine how we will respond. "It is not simply what has happened to them that has defined them; their responses to what has happened to them have been of even greater importance, and these responses have been shaped by their interpretations of what they suffered."[3] "It is in the response to suffering that many and perhaps all men, individually and in their groups, define themselves, take on character, develop their ethos."[4] What matters most is not what has happened to you; what matters most is what you will do now.

Viktor Frankl was a German psychiatrist who found himself in a Nazi prison camp. His observations of the behaviors of other prisoners led to the classic book *In Search of Meaning*. Frankl found that the way prisoners responded to their adversity dramatically decided their outcome—even resulting in quick death. Peter Kreeft offers this quote of Frankl:

> Do the prisoner's reactions to the singular world of the concentration camp prove that man cannot escape the influences of his surroundings? Does man have no choice of action in the face of such circumstances?
>
> We can answer these questions from experience as well as on principle. The experiences of camp life show that man does have a choice of action. There were enough examples, often of a heroic nature, which proved that apathy could be overcome.... Man *can* preserve a vestige of spiritual freedom,

2. Neibuhr, *Responsible Ethic*, 172–73.
3. Ibid., 59.
4. Ibid., 60.

of independence of mind, even in such terrible conditions of psychic and physical stress."[5]

You cannot control a lot of the things that happen to you. But you cannot blame your situation for the decisions you make. What you do from here is your decision alone.

Yancey argues that we have a lot of control in determining our tolerance of pain. One factor that makes suffering more intolerable is a sense of helplessness. Maintaining a sense of hope is vital to enduring suffering. Transferring one's attention from one's own plight to the suffering of others often reduces the pain.[6] Sitting around whining about our dilemma provides some satisfaction, but no real relief. It may well seem easiest to just throw up our hands in despair over the impossibilities that lie before us. Or we can find hope in God and push through the darkness to a new tomorrow. And we can notice that we are not the only one in pain and take whatever action is in our power to help someone else enjoying the satisfaction of caring for another.

You have to decide what will come of this. Will it all be a loss? Or will you grow because of it?

> The supreme challenge to anyone facing catastrophic loss involves facing the darkness of the loss on the one hand, and learning to live with renewed vitality and gratitude on the other. This challenge is met when we learn to take the loss into ourselves and to be enlarged by it, so that our capacity to live life well and to know God intimately increases. To escape the loss is far less healthy—and far less realistic, considering how devastating loss can be—than to grow from it. Loss can diminish us, but it can also expand us. It depends, once again, on the

---

5. As quoted in Kreeft, *Making Sense Out of Suffering*, 73.
6. Yancey, *Where Is God When It Hurts?*, 137–56.

choices we make and the grace we receive. Loss can function as a catalyst to transform us. It can lead us to God, the only One who has the desire and power to give us life.[7]

Many are finding recovery and freedom through twelve-step programs like Alcoholics Anonymous. Basic to these programs is recognition that the person's addiction is a kind of disability, yet the individual is required to make right choices. Life is not fair, but this offers no excuse. You must decide what you will do next. You probably cannot make the changes alone, but you must do what you can. Get up and walk.

God has created us as free moral agents, and he invites us to join him in partnership. As Richard Rice says, "What God decides to do depends on what people decide to do."[8] We decide with God what the future will be—at least our own future. It is our duty as free moral agents to resist evil. We must not surrender to evil, complaining that it is God's will; we must rise up in protest to overcome that which God does not will. It may be evil within us that we must combat. It may be that we must take arms against evil systems in our world that cause us and others pain and suffering. This is our mission, to bring about the will of God by fighting against evil.

It may be that part of the action you need to take is forgiveness. There may have been another person that has done you wrong and brought you into your current condition. You must choose between nursing resentment against them as you dig deeper into your hole or letting it go and moving on with your life.

The process of forgiveness begins when victims realize that nothing—not justice or revenge or anything else—can

---

7. Sittser, *Grace Disguised*, 180–81.
8. Rice, "Biblical Support for a New Position," 32.

reverse the wrong done. Forgiveness cannot spare victims the consequences of the loss, nor can it recover the life they once had. Victims have no power to change the past. No one can bring the dead back to life or erase the horror of a rape or pay back squandered investments. In the case of catastrophic loss, what has happened is done. There is no going back.

But there can be going ahead. Victims can choose life instead of death. They can choose to stop the cycle of destruction and, in the wake of the wrong done, do what is right. Forgiveness is simply choosing to do the right thing. It heals instead of hurts, restores broken relationships, and substitutes love where there was hate. Though forgiveness seems to contradict what seems fair and right, forgiving people decide that they would rather live in a merciful universe than in a fair one, for their sake as much as for anyone else's. Life is mean enough as it is; they choose not to make it any meaner.[9]

In order to do what is required, you will surely need God's help. We discussed in the previous chapter that God cares about you. God's Holy Spirit is available to you as a Comforter and to empower you for victorious living. You do not have to act alone. God's grace is already given. You must avail yourself of the power offered by the Holy Spirit to do what you have to do.

9. Sittser, *Grace Disguised*, 125–26.

Questions for Discussion

1. Why do we so often attempt to project responsibility on someone other than ourselves?

2. Discuss the role of the Holy Spirit in empowering believers for victorious living.

3. How have you found joy in overcoming life's struggles?

4. What challenges face you today? What are you going to do to apply these principles?

Section 3

A Primer on Theodicy

Chapter 7

A Symphony of Perspectives

In this section, we will delve a little more deeply into the issues of theodicy. Those who want truly in-depth philosophical discussion are referred to other sources as listed in the bibliography. But we will consider some of the most important foundational issues and some of the implications that follow. The reader is advised that the writing style will change from that of the first chapters. Until now, we have used a style designed to be accessible to most readers and targeted to people who are challenged with the tragedies of life discussing certain ideas common among Christians. This section will dig a little deeper into theological and philosophical thought to explore the issues already discussed. You may be wondering whether the ideas discussed so far have any credibility. The fact is that much serious thought runs counter to the popular perceptions held by many Christians. Actually, this book offers nothing new or creative but is a restatement of the best of classic Christian thought. In this section, you may need to use a dictionary to define unfamiliar vocabulary. You will find more frequent footnotes, often offering leads to other scholars you may choose to read. This section offers a summary for those who are not inclined to read dozens of books to answer the questions raised by the tragedies of life. You may find that the previous chapters provide all you need and will choose to read no further. Before putting the book away, you might check the final section that is not so academic where you can find practical helps. For those who want more, a quick course on the philosophy of suffering is offered in the following four chapters.

As we introduced earlier, theodicy presents a three-way riddle, or Triadox, contrasting the belief that God is omnipotent, God is perfectly good (or loving), and evil is a reality. One of the earliest thinkers to frame a modern analysis of the problem of suffering was David Hume. This skeptical philosopher believed he could eliminate the possibility of God, saying, "Is he willing to prevent evil, but not able? then he is impotent. Is he able, but not willing? then he is malevolent. Is he both able and willing? whence, then is evil?"[1] For many, this question is the proof that Christianity is false. If we cannot answer the question of suffering, we really have nothing else to talk about. Ah, but the Truth of our faith shines through the challenge of theodicy.

Discussion of theodicy often becomes more widespread in response to particularly heinous examples of evil or suffering. A historic event was the 1750 Lisbon earthquake, which killed thousands attending mass, which provoked the Voltaire farce *Candide*. The slave trade that supported the economy of the early United States provides grist for discussion of our inhumanity to each other. Nothing in the twentieth century is better evidence of moral evil than the Holocaust of Nazi Germany. Many were horrified by the injustice of flying jetliners into the World Trade Center towers on September 11, 2001. The destructive power of natural forces was displayed in the tsunami that destroyed villages in Indonesia and Thailand in December 2004, in Hurricane Katrina in August 2005, and in the earthquake that devastated Haiti in January 2010. More mundane realities like the killing of one animal by another to maintain the food chain are ever-present topics for consideration. Do these ugly realities disprove the Christian message of a God who rules over all and who loves his children?

---

1. Hume, *Dialogues Concerning Natural Religion*, 198. Hume's riddle dates to Epicurus.

Discussions on theodicy over the last millennia tend to address certain common themes.[2] Some must be discarded as unacceptable to Christian faith. Some are helpful in conjunction with other themes. Most have some point of exception, so complete consensus has not been achieved around any solution.

The Triadox can be resolved by denying either the power of God, the love of God, or the reality of evil. Some are convinced that the problem of evil is unsolvable and that the only answer is to deny the existence of God or to postulate that evil is a power that is equal to God. This solution is not acceptable to Christian faith and is more attuned to the ancient religion of Manichaeism. Some would assert that God is not good, but is malicious. Any explanation that God deliberately wills our suffering is reprehensible for Christian theodicy. Some solve the problem by denying the reality of evil, seeing it as an allusion. This also is an unsatisfactory solution.

Within the mainstream of Christian theodicy are solutions that clarify one or more aspects of the Triadox. Some affirm the omnipotence of God while asserting that even an all-powerful God has certain limits of rationality (we will explore this in the next chapter). Some affirm the love of God while asserting that there are reasons beyond our understanding that would explain why a loving God would allow things that we view as evil. While the God of the Bible certainly rules over all, to say that "God allows this to happen" opens a Pandora's box for theodicy. Some follow Leibniz in asserting that this is "the best possible world." This conclusion is reached by deduction starting with the assumption of God: since God is all-powerful and is good, then it logically follows that what God created must be right. Others follow the Augustinian argument that evil is not a thing that God created

---

2. I would like to acknowledge the discussions offered by others to summarize the options in Christian theodicy: Vieth, *Holy Power, Human Pain* 25–55; Oden, *Pastoral Theology*, 227–236; Davis, "Holocaust and the Problem of Theodicy."

but is a privation of good. Following this line of thought, we can assert that the way to avoid grieving is to never have loved.

Some argue that suffering is a matter of divine retribution: God's punishment on evil or disobedience. This kind of thinking can be found in the Bible. Some would extend this to argue that the Holocaust was punishment on the Jews. This theory is certainly open to charges of anti-Semitism. It takes a stretch to use Deuteronomy 28 to indict modern Judaism of idolatry.

Some attribute evil and suffering to Satan and avoid dualism by asserting that Satan is created by God and accountable to God, but acting in rebellion. Satan is a popular foil, but many beliefs about Satan go beyond sound biblical interpretation. John Milton's *Paradise Lost* is sometimes more formative than anything in the Bible.

Some (including this author) find the answer in free will. The argument is that the greatest good is that God granted freedom to creation rather than ordaining that all things respond in obedience to the will of God. Discussions of free will can extend not only to human decision but to the natural order.

Some limit the power of God saying that there is nothing God could do to prevent evil. This seems to some to be a denial of the omnipotence of God and thus is a refutation of biblical theism. The recent developments of process theology and open theism (discussed in chapter ten) assert that God's power does not include knowledge of the future and the future is yet to be decided and therefore is unknowable.

Some argue that there may be some good in what we view as evil. Some see suffering as a test from God designed to prove our faith or an ordeal designed to help us to reach a goal. Some affirm biblical theism but resign themselves to a mystery or the inscrutability of God. They might argue that the problem is rooted in our limited perspective: if we could see the big picture we would understand why things are the way they are. Maybe the problem is that we are not spiritually capable of receiving all of God's goodness.

Some discuss the phenomenon that individual suffering is socially rooted and socially redeemed. We are not alone. We suffer because of the sins of others, and others suffer because of our sins. Through the cross, Christ has established a people, a new community in which we find salvation.

Some discussion addresses issues other than the origin of evil or suffering. Some find hope in the assertion that God's power can draw good out of any evil. Sometimes we have to wait a long time to realize what the good is. Many natural disasters are part of a healthy process. Some assert that evil does not limit God's power. In fact, it is a testimony to God's power that he can tolerate such diversity. The truly mature parent loves the child enough to let them loose. It is the dysfunctional parent who manipulates the child. Suffering and even hell are testimony to God's great love for us. God continues to manifest his power in the ongoing pursuit of us. Some discuss the benefits of suffering. Suffering can be a healing medicine—a laxative. Burning your hand teaches you to respect fire. We often become more effective in ministering to others because of pain we have experienced. But suffering does have an effect of teaching us. Discipline is here more like exercise or working out (no pain, no gain) than punishment. Some emphasize the growth that often results from suffering. The moth cannot survive without the struggle of escaping the cocoon. Complacency or stagnancy are not good. Some discuss the way that suffering may put goodness in bolder relief. In music, dissonance resolves to harmony. If we never knew sorrow, would we really appreciate joy? In each of these discussions, evil and suffering are perceived as having some beneficial outcomes.

Philip Yancey offers a very helpful discussion on the problem of suffering in his book *Disappointment with God: Three Questions No One Asks Aloud*. Yancey's three questions are: (1) Is God unfair? Why doesn't he consistently punish evil people and reward good people? Why do awful things happen to people good and bad, with no discernable pattern? (2) Is God silent? If he is so concerned about our doing his will, why doesn't he reveal that more plainly? And, (3) Is God hidden? Why doesn't he simply show up sometime, visibly, and dumbfound the skeptics once and for all? Yancey addresses his second question referring to the Exodus story as evidence that it doesn't help for God to speak plainly. He concludes, "The Israelites give ample proof that signs may only addict us to signs, not to God."[3]

Yancey outlines four options often considered in response to the difficult questions of life:

1. Life is not fair and neither is God.
2. Life is unfair but God can't do much about it.
3. Life is unfair but God will even the score in the next life.
4. The world is fair. Stop complaining.

He then suggests that the best answer is that life is unfair, but that doesn't mean God is unfair. The question is based in the assumption that life equals God, so that the fact that life is unfair proves that God is unfair. But the existence and love of God are not conditioned on our health or prosperity. Those saints who live victorious over trials have discovered that their relationship with God must be independent of their temporal existence.[4]

Yancey advances sage ponderings to counter the questions of doubt that we experience when facing the tragedies of life. "Perhaps God keeps us ignorant because enlightenment might not help us."[5] "Perhaps God keeps us ignorant because we are

---

3. Yancey, *Disappointment with God*, 44–48. Richard Swinburne points out that if God kept bailing us out, we would become dependent (Swinburne, *Existence of God*, 210–11).

4. Yancey, *Disappointment with God*, 179–80.

5. Ibid., 191.

incapable of comprehending the answer."[6] "The kind of faith God values seems to develop best when everything fuzzes over, when God stays silent, when the fog rolls in."[7] After all his discussion, Yancey suggests there is one thing that would be worse than disappointment with God, and that would be disappointment *without* God.[8] Life may be difficult, but the wise must find a way to overcome the challenges. Among the greatest challenges is coping with questions for which we have not found satisfactory answers.

This discussion of theodicy works within certain parameters of Christian belief, although across the ages many philosophers have attempted to discuss theodicy apart from traditional Christian faith. Both Christian and non-Christian philosophers have sought to prove logically that there is a God[9] and then explain evil and suffering within that logical construct. But God's existence is an assumed foundation of Christian faith. Some suggest that evil is nothing more than a matter of perspective:[10] But evil, pain, and suffering[11] are unavoidable aspects of life. If we accept the notion that there is a God who is all-powerful and loving and we confront the reality of evil, then we are left with the Christian dilemma of reconciling divine sovereignty with free will. Some Christians assume that if God is Lord of All, then everything that

---

6. Ibid., 193.

7. Ibid., 204.

8. Ibid., 184.

9. Thomas Aquinas, Immanuel Kant, etc.

10. Besides the Christian Science invented by Mary Baker Eddy, Buddhism takes a similar approach to the problem of evil. Some forms of postmodernism take similar approaches. (Stackhouse, *Can God Be Trusted?*, 24–26). I will be discussing some aspects of perspective and perception as I see their relevance.

11. I tend to lump these concepts together as though they are synonymous. I recognize that they are not and leave it to others to explore these nuances of meaning. Hick delineates the difference between pain and suffering. Pain was once considered the opposite of pleasure. Pain is not seen as a physical sensation that has no opposite. The opposite of pleasure is suffering. Pain leads to suffering, although suffering can come without physical pain (Hick, *Evil and the God of Love*, 292).

happens must be at his directive:[12] A better course is to explore
the implications of free will. Can we maintain a belief that God is
all-powerful and perfect in all his ways while also confronting the
ugliness of our existence? We can and we must. We cannot do that
by saying that God caused these things to happen for some reason.

---

12. Popular writers of recent years include Kay Arthur, *When Bad Things Happen*;
James Dobson Jr., *When God Doesn't Make Sense*; and Joni Eareckson Tada, *When
God Weeps: Why Our Sufferings Matter to the Almighty*. While I have deep respect for
the devotion to God and his Word these persons represent, I am convinced that their
convictions are rooted more in a particular theological tradition than in reality.

Chapter 8

The Core Issues

Theodicy is a complex issue that requires more than simplistic thought. Some begin with the idea that God is Lord of all and reach conclusions that are logically consistent with that basis but that fail to address the realities of life. In this chapter, we will consider what limitations might exist for an all-powerful or omnipotent God. In the process we must also consider the implications of free will or choice.

Can we recognize that the power of God has certain limits without denying God himself? This is an area much discussed by philosophers when wrestling with the issue of theodicy. There is no denial of God's omnipotence or sovereignty in recognizing the limits to his ability. This is a simple matter of rationality. As Richard Swinburne reminds us, God cannot make two teams win the same game.[1]

Discussions on this truth usually reference the statements of Thomas Aquinas, one of the greatest theologians in the history of the church. He declared, "God can do all things that are possible."[2] He went on to state, "Whatever implies contradiction does not come within the scope of the omnipotence of God."[3] The skeptic can try to spin riddles about God making a rock so big that even

---

1. Swinburne, *Providence and the Problem of Evil,* 125–26.
2. Aquinas, *Summa Theologica,* IaQ, XXV, Art. 3.
3. Ibid., Art. 4.

he cannot move it. But this does not prove anything. God is not disproved by nonsense. God can do anything that can be done.

C. S. Lewis wrote one of the most popular books of the twentieth century on this subject. Lewis declared, "His omnipotence means the power to do all that is intrinsically possible, not to do the intrinsically impossible."[4] We will discuss the issue of free will further. Lewis says, "Not even Omnipotence could create a society of free souls without at the same time creating a relatively independent and 'inexorable' Nature."[5] Later, he says, "Try to exclude the possibility of suffering which the order of nature and the existence of free wills involve, and you will find that you have excluded life itself."[6] With his unique flair with language, Lewis offered this in response to the idea presented by Leibniz that this is "the best of all possible worlds":

> Perhaps this is not the "best of all possible universes," but the only possible one. Possible worlds can mean only "worlds that God could have made but didn't." The idea of that which God "could have" done involves a too anthropomorphic conception of God's freedom. Whatever human freedom means, Divine freedom cannot mean Indeterminacy between alternatives and choice of one of them. Perfect goodness can never debate about the end to be attained, and perfect wisdom cannot debate about the means most suited to achieve it. The freedom of God consists of the fact that no cause other than Himself produces His acts and no external obstacle impedes them—that His own goodness is the root from which they all grow and His own omnipotence the air in which they all flower.[7]

---

4. Lewis, *Problem of Pain*, 28.
5. Ibid., 29.
6. Ibid., 34.
7. Ibid., 35.

Whatever tangents we may take in philosophical speculation, our theodicy must remain grounded in the reality of who God is and what is possible.

I have never heard anyone argue that God can change the past. The fact that God cannot rewrite history does not limit his omnipotence in any way. God can do anything that can be done.

S. Paul Schilling wrote a recent treatise attempting a practical treatment of the issue of theodicy. He adds this description of the logical *non sequiter* of denying God because we find that there are limits to his omnipotence.

> Just as he cannot make a spherical cube, he cannot create a world in which his rational creatures are both free to choose the right and incapable of wrong. If he determined their thoughts and actions for them, they would not be moral agents but marionettes possessing no intrinsic worth, God sets the abstract limits within which persons function, but within these limits he sets them free to make their own decisions, incorporating in his universe the results of their actions and thereby giving them permanent meaning. These provisions involve dangerous risks—for God as well as for his creatures.[8]

Schilling also provides a wonderful refutation to the argument that evil somehow invalidates the goodness of God.

> Orthodox Christian thought has traditionally asserted the omnipotence as well as the perfect goodness of God. Ordinarily, thinkers who have affirmed both have recognized that the divine power is limited by whatever measure of freedom God has allotted to his creatures. However, this limitation is

---

8. Schilling, *God and Human Anguish*, 201–2.

regarded as willed by God himself in order to facilitate the growth of persons fashioned in his image. Since it is self-imposed, it is under his control and subject to revocation by his own choice. Hence it is felt to be quite consistent with divine omnipotence. It can be maintained also that the regularity and uniformity of the natural order and the social and cosmic interdependence of the created world do not necessarily represent a diminution of God's power, since these provisions may be regarded as chosen by God as the best means of fulfilling his loving purpose.[9]

God is able to do whatever God chooses to do. Part of God's choice is to give us freedom. God could have done otherwise: God could have created a universe where all things move at his direction in perfection. This would be a scripted world of puppets, very different from the world of authentic relationships God desired. Yancey reminds us that God's decision to create autonomous creatures presents a limit in itself, much as an artist is limited by their choice of medium. If the artist chooses to paint with oils, there are limits on what they can accomplish. If the artist chooses to sculpt with clay, they again face certain limits. Should the artist choose to use a camera, they still face the limitations of that media. "By a commitment to human freedom, God imposed certain limits on himself. Whenever a creator enters a certain medium, he is limited by that medium."[10] Elsewhere, Yancey says, "Creation involves a kind of self-limiting."[11] God could have done otherwise, but in his wisdom and love, he chose to take this route.

Perhaps the most definitive philosophical treatment of the issue of theodicy and the free will defense of the last century is that of Alvin Plantinga. Plantinga works through a long list of logical

---

9. Ibid., 236.
10. Yancey, *Where Is God*, 54.
11. Yancey, *Disappointment with God*, 59.

syllogisms (equations) to show that there is no inconsistency with the Great Trilemma.[12] Another great theodicist of our time is John Hick, who says of Plantinga:

> In his treatment of the problems of evil, Alvin Plantinga confines his reasonings to the paths of formal logic. He is concerned to determine what can and cannot be strictly proved or disproved in this area. Such a procedure limits him to a narrow but precisely defined issue, namely whether (as has been alleged by some philosophers), there is a logical contradiction between the proposition that "an omnipotent, omniscient and wholly good God exists" and the proposition that "evil exists." If there were such a logical contradiction it would generate a strict disproof of divine existence, at least as this is conceived in Christianity. And Plantinga's technically superb arguments are largely confined to showing that no such strict disproof is possible because the alleged logical contradiction on which it relies does not exist.[13]

Some go so far as the assert that Plantinga has closed the discussion by proving that there is no logical contradiction in the Great Triadox.

William Willimon, former dean of the chapel for Duke University, offers this summation of the problem of rejecting the omnipotence of God based on limits that we have found in his power.

> Most theodicy doesn't work because it begins with ideals or abstract standards of what ought to be. It demands that God ought to be "omnipotent" by our standards of power, "good" by our definitions of goodness. Invariably, the end result is

---

12. Plantinga, *God, Freedom and Evil*; see also Plantinga, *Nature of Necessity*.
13. Hick, *Evil and the God of Love*, 365–66.

not congruent with the story of the One who has "borne our griefs and carried our sorrows."[14]

I want to build on this in the next chapter.

Believing that we have a free will and are responsible for our choices is not contrary to the sovereignty of God. Augustine, the church father on whom all Christian discussion of the free will defense is based, said, "Free will is the cause of our doing evil."[15] We have to ask, what kind of freedom would it be if God did not allow us to do wrong or to suffer the consequences? Gregory Boyd argues, "Creation doesn't have to have *actual* evil, but it must allow for the *possibility* of evil—if the possibility of genuine love is to exist."[16] Boyd goes on to say, "Life is arbitrary because of the way the decisions made by an unfathomably vast multitude of free agents intersect with each other. It is not a function of God's will or character."[17] By choosing to establish free will, God restricted his ability to intervene.[18] Schilling says, "It is widely held that at least limited freedom is essential to the existence and fulfillment of life on a truly personal level, but that this provision inevitably leads to suffering when freedom is deliberately, carelessly, or ignorantly misused."[19] Schilling explains that free will does not mean indeterminism as choices are conditioned by a number of factors other than God's direct control. The statement "everything happens for a reason" has an element of truth. Much of what we experience in life has a certain cause and effect. But these causes are often multiple and not always obvious. We should be wary of attributing the ultimate cause to the will of God.

---

14. Willimon, *Sighing for Eden*, 83.

15. Augustine, *Augustine: Confessions and Enchiridion*, 137.

16. Boyd, *Is God to Blame?*, 63. Boyd will be discussed later as a proponent of the open view of God.

17. Ibid., 108.

18. Ibid., 111–13.

19. Schilling, *God and Human Anguish*, 93–194.

As we discussed in chapter three, Augustine provides a foundation for much of Christian theology, particularly the understanding of theodicy. It was Augustine who argued so definitively that evil is not a created thing. Rather, evil is the privation of the good that God intends. Often quoted are these words from the great Augustine.

For what is that which we call evil but the absence of good?[20]

Just in the same way, what are called vices in the soul are nothing but privations of natural good.[21]

Nothing evil exists *in itself.*[22]

God judged it better to bring good out of evil than not to permit evil to exist.[23]

The analogies of light and darkness, hot and cold, sound and silence[24] should illustrate the reality that evil is not among the things God created but rather is the result of the freedom that God allows to all creation. Evil is never God's will. The only alternative to evil is a world carefully ordered by God's perfect will, a world devoid of any meaningful relationship. This world would not only be devoid of relationship but of personhood itself. This was not God's design. God desired that we be free creatures so that he could enjoy a mutual loving relationship with us. This truly is "the best possible world," to use the description coined by Leibniz. But it comes at the price of evil, pain, and suffering when we choose other than God's perfect will.

---

20. Augustine, *Augustine: Confessions and Enchiridion*, 342. See also http://www.tertullian.org/fathers/augustine_enchiridion_02_trans.htm.

21. Ibid.

22. Ibid., 344.

23. Ibid., 355.

24. See chapter 4 if you do not recognize this allusion.

Chapter 9

Is God a Stage Manager?

Much of our discussion of theodicy is a matter of perception and perspective. The assumptions we begin with tend to predetermine our conclusions. Merle Strege says that theodicy is a product of the Enlightenment.[1] Surin says that most theodicists (like Swinburne) are basing their work on a non-Christian god produced by the Enlightenment.[2] This is not the Trinitarian God of Christianity. How we view the problem determines our outcome. People used to think that fire was an evil to be combated vigorously. The result was the massive forest fires of the 1980s. We have learned that fire plays a constructive role in building forests. Many see the grey wolf as a nuisance and want to kill them to protect cattle, sheep, and children. But wolves play a constructive role in maintaining the balance of ecology.

The meaning of evil cannot be understood apart from its relationship to good. We regard as good those experiences that we desire, cherish, and seek to conserve and enhance; as evil those that we try to avoid because they impair attainment of goods or values. Normatively, *good* refers to experiences that

---

1. Strege was one of my seminary professors and is an ethicist, theologian, and the historian of the Church of God (Anderson, Indiana). He mentioned this in discussion of my book during a breakfast conversation on June 29, 2007.

2. Surin, *Theology and the Problem of Evil*, 3–7.

are really desirable because they enrich and fulfill life, while *evil* refers to those that thwart such fulfillment and impede the actualization of value. It is not easy to distinguish between real and apparent goods and evils, though we dare never forget that events perceived as evil by the one experiencing them must be treated seriously because they are evil for him.[3]

It may well be that some of the suffering that we regard as evil may be a part of a good process. But because we find something not to our liking, we call it evil. Is this not the ultimate of idolatry, where we project ourselves into the place of God and insist that our perception is truth? Maybe the problem is our lack of understanding.

What does it mean that God is sovereign? Many discussions on theodicy make the simple statement, "If God is all-powerful, then he must be able to prevent evil." Are we capable of defining the power of God in such a way that does not deny the reality of who he is and what he can do? C. S. Lewis said, "If God is wiser than we his judgment must differ from ours on many things, and not least on good and evil. What seems to us good may therefore not be good in his eyes, and what seems to us evil may not be evil."[4] Because God is so different from us, we cannot begin to evaluate his goodness.

> What would really satisfy us would be a God who said of anything we happened to like doing, "What does it matter as long as they are contented?" We want, in fact, not so much a Father in Heaven as a grandfather in heaven—a senile benevolence who, as they say "liked to see young people enjoying themselves, and whose plan for the universe was simply that it might be truly said at the end of each day, 'a good time was had by all.'"[5]

---

3. Schilling, *God and Human Anguish*, 10.
4. Lewis, *Problem of Pain*, 37.
5. Ibid., 40.

There are difficult questions to be answered as we experience the tragedies of life. But at some point, we must recognize that our demands for answers are much like that of children who know not what is good for them but who throw tantrums because their parents do not satisfy their whims. God does not have to answer to us. He is sovereign. At the same time, all his ways are just, if we can only begin to understand what justice is.

What is required in the holiness of God? Many discussions on theodicy argue, if God is good (or loving), then he would do something about our problems. Is God lacking in goodness because he does not do everything the way we demand? Like children, we accuse our Father of not loving us because we do not get our way.

> What in effect the objection is asking is that a God should make a toy-world, a world where things matter, but not very much; where we can choose and our choices can make a small difference, but the real choices remain God's. For he simply would not allow us the choice of doing real harm, or through our negligence allowing harm to occur. He would be like the over-protective parent who will not let his child out of his sight for a moment.[6]

God is no dysfunctional parent. He truly allows his children to have a loose leash. He does not protect us at every point from the consequences of our choices. He has set us free to enjoy the heights of maturity along with the depths of depravity. God is not to be blamed for the outcome of our freedom.

Are we sure that suffering is always a bad thing? Many discussions on theodicy are based in the assumption that evil, pain, and suffering are, by definition, inconsistent with the power and love

---

6. Swinburne, *Existence of God*, 219–20.

of God. But is this true? We usually understand that while recovering from corrective surgery, we must endure discomfort and pain. Yancey illustrates this point with a discussion of Hansen's disease (leprosy) and other diseases (diabetes, drug addiction) that provide examples of the destructive effect of a life without pain sensors.[7] It doesn't take a great deal of imagination to comprehend that suffering is often a productive part of life. Most of us have reflected on ways that we have grown as a result of suffering. We will discuss later the way that John Hick focuses on the constructive use of suffering for soul-making. Hick challenges Hume's objection that God should have created a world without pain, showing how a world without pain would offer no motivation to resolve hunger or to strive for excellence.[8]

Another aspect of perception concerns consideration of the perspective of God. We tend to be preoccupied with our own perspective, as if that is the only viewpoint. How does God experience the tragedies of life? Does God suffer? Classic Christian theology is often based on Greek philosophical thinking that God must be unchangeable (impassible). Jürgen Moltmann offers a helpful discussion of the biblical God of compassion in contrast with the impassible god of the philosophers.

> Were God incapable of suffering in any respect, and therefore in an absolute sense, then he would also be incapable of love. If love is the acceptance of the other without regard to one's own well-being, then it contains within itself the possibility of sharing in suffering and freedom to suffer as a result of the otherness of the other. Incapability of suffering in this sense would contradict the fundamental Christian assertion that God is love, which in principle broke the spell of the

---

7. Yancey, *Where Is God*, 31–39; see also Sittser, *Grace Disguised*, 46.
8. Hick, *Evil and the God of Love*, 304–9.

Aristotelian doctrine of God. The one who is capable of love is also capable of suffering, for he also opens himself to the suffering which is involved in love, and yet remains superior to it by virtue of his love.[9]

Moltmann quotes the oft-cited story from Elie Weisel about God being present in the Holocaust, saying: "To speak here of a God who could not suffer would make God a demon. To speak here of an absolute God would make God an annihilating nothingness. To speak here of an indifferent God would condemn men to indifference."[10] The God of the Bible is a God of compassion who responds to the suffering of his people.

Some Christians are convinced that if God is sovereign, then he must have decided on everything that happens. Some would go so far as to say there is no free will, that God determines everything. Others see beyond such mechanistic thinking, but insist that while humans have free will, God must have created a world where they freely choose to do the right thing. The Christian can believe that God is sovereign over all things without believing that God determines all things.[11] Beyond the limits of rationality that we have already discussed, there are reasons for eschewing the concept of determinism. Does God control even what we think? Even the Calvinist affirms that we are responsible for moral choices. They simply insist that all are guilty of sin but God determines who is forgiven apart from our choice.

While much popular Christian literature purports a simplistic view that everything that happens is the result of God's control, there are plenty of serious scholars who offer other viewpoints. Gregory Boyd says, "We have no reason to assume there is a particular divine reason behind every instance of suffering we

9. Moltmann, *Crucified God*, 230.
10. Ibid., 273–74.
11. I discuss the issue of determinism in my book *Are You Sure You're Right?*

confront."[12] David Biebel says, "God is not the Author of evil and cannot be held responsible for the actions or consequences of evil people. Nor can the responsibility for genetic illnesses, disease, and death be laid at His feet, except in that He created man like Himself, a free moral agent."[13] Leslie Weatherhead says, "We have got to get out of our heads the notion that everything that happens occurs because God wants it that way."[14] Barry Whitney says, "It is unacceptable to postulate that each and every evil fulfills some specific purpose for good ends. Clearly there are evils which lead not to good ends but to even greater evils. The distribution of evil, moreover, is so apparently unjust that any belief that it is deliberately caused by God for specific ends seems religiously, morally, and intellectually offensive."[15] David Bentley Hart, writing in the wake of the tsunami that wiped out villages around the Indian Ocean on Christmas 2005, offered this:

> This idea of a God who can be called omnipotent only if his will is the direct efficient cause of every aspect of created reality immediately makes all the inept cavils of the village atheist seem profound: one still should not ask if God could create a stone he could not lift, perhaps, but one might legitimately ask if a God of infinite voluntaristic sovereignty and power could create a creature free to resist the divine will. The question is no cruder than the conception of God it is meant to mock, and the paradox thus produced merely reflects the deficiencies of that conception.
>
> Frankly, any understanding of divine sovereignty so unsubtle that it requires the theologian to assert (as Calvin

---

12. Boyd, *Is God to Blame?*, 84.
13. Biebel, *If God Is So Good*, 141.
14. As quoted in Willimon, *Sighing for Eden*, 65.
15. Whitney, *Evil and the Process God*, 139. While this is a good quote, I must distance myself from the process orientation of its context.

did) that God foreordained the fall of humanity so that his glory might be revealed in the predestined damnation of the derelict is obviously problematic, and probably far more blasphemous than anything represented by the heresies that the ancient ecumenical councils confronted."[16]

Philip Yancey declares, "Suffering is not a direct act of God which we must swallow as a punishment."[17] Later, he offers this thought, "Maybe God *isn't trying to tell us anything specific* each time we hurt. Pain and suffering are part and parcel of our planet, and Christians are not exempt."[18] Popular Christian thinking asserts that there must be a reason. More sophisticated analysis reaches awareness that life is far more complex, that much of what we experience cannot be easily explained by ascribing it to the sovereignty of God.

Some will ask, "Don't you believe that God allows these things to happen?" What does it mean to say that God allows evil? If God is truly sovereign over all things, he could have made a different creation. But God did not will that all things be under his direct control. He surrendered his sovereignty in the interest of choice. As stated by Clark Pinnock, "God is a superior power who does not cling to his right to dominate and control but who voluntarily gives creatures room to flourish. By inviting them to have dominion over the world (for example), God willingly surrenders power and makes possible a partnership with the creature."[19] Not only did God give freedom to those he created in his image, but he also gave a sense of freedom to all living things and nonanimate things. This freedom was certainly allowed by God. But this does not connote that God signs off on some cosmic checklist of every

16. Christian Century, "Where Was God?"

17. Yancey, *Where Is God*, 72.

18. Ibid., 67.

19. Pinnock, *Openness of God*, 113. Rabbi Harold Kushner (*When Bad Things Happen*, 29–30) and others take a different position saying that God is unable to do anything about evil, limiting omnipotence.

detail of our lives. If by "everything happens for a reason," we mean that there is usually a cause and effect to everything, that is one thing, but we should not expect that everything that happens fits the divine purpose. Thus, the assertion, life is not fair.

If evil is God's will, then should we not accept it? Isn't this the same as the doctrine of *karma* advocated by Hinduism and new age religions? Our duty is to resist evil, not resign to it as God's will. Christianity has led the way in fighting evil, whether through hospitals or orphanages or abolitionism or any of the other ways that we have sought to counter the force of evil in history. This glorious reality is based in the biblical revelation that all things are not the outworking of God's will. We live in a broken world where much is in defiance of God's intention. Our calling is to work toward the extension of the kingdom of God to all creation. We have every right to protest pain and suffering, in fact it is our duty to work to overcome evil.

While the issue of moral evil is difficult, discussion of natural evil is even more baffling. Why do bad things happen that have no apparent connection to human behavior? Every year, we hear of an earthquake, fire, hurricane, or some other natural disaster that wreaks death and destruction. How do we explain all of this? Could it be that God has not only granted free will to humans but also to all creation? The issue of freedom is discussed by some as indeterminacy: even the natural order is free to do the wrong thing. Paul Tillich says, "Physical evil is the natural implication of creaturely finitude. Moral evil is the tragic implication of creaturely freedom."[20] Events commonly described as "acts of God" are more accurately perceived as outworking of natural forces. In some cases, we can see evidence that human misdeeds have produced

---

20. Tillich, *Systematic Theology*, 167. Tillich, among others, says that God gave freedom to the natural order. This provides an alternative to saying that sin caused natural evil. After all, carnivorous animals surely predated the Fall. This is part of a discussion of determinism within a discussion on freedom and destiny (Ibid., 184–86).

damage to the natural order; but much natural evil cannot be attributed to sin. It is the consequence of our condition.[21] Physics has found a randomness (Principle of Indeterminancy) where once was seen "laws of nature."[22]

Schilling gives an especially capable discussion to the reality of natural evil. He shows that while God is the primary cause of all things, freedom exists not only among people but in all creation to do other than the best.[23] Schilling discusses the idea of maintaining divine control of free creatures as something like hypnotic suggestion. He shows how such creatures could not rise to goodness or initiative any more than can computers.[24] Schilling discusses the lack of determination at the atomic level as has been discussed from the ancient philosopher Epicurus up to quantum physics and the Heisenberg principle.[25] He also explores the interrelatedness of creation and its implications for suffering unrelated to one's own actions.[26]

Still, we can affirm the biblical assertions that some aspects of natural evil are consequences of human misconduct. The Augustinian paradigm was that God created all things in perfection and that we damaged this perfection with our sin. In the Genesis account, God says to man, "Cursed is the ground because of you; through painful toil you will eat of it all the days of your life. It will produce thorns and thistles for you, and you will eat the plants of the field" (Gen 3:17–18). The clear implication is that God willed that we enjoy a perfect garden where all our needs were provided, but we negated that option and brought pain to all creation. In his great soliloquy, Paul proclaimed,

---

21. Yancey, *Where Is God*, 71.

22. Vieth, *Holy Power, Human Pain*, 32.

23. Schilling, *God and Human Anguish*, 202.

24. Ibid., 206–7. This idea was discussed earlier by renowned atheist Anthony Flew in Flew, "Divine Omnipotence and Human Freedom," 161–68.

25. Ibid., 209–13.

26. Ibid., 215–25.

I consider that our present sufferings are not worth comparing with the glory that will be revealed in us. The creation waits in eager expectation for the sons of God to be revealed. For the creation was subjected to frustration, not by its own choice, but by the will of the one who subjected it, in hope that the creation itself will be liberated from its bondage to decay and brought into the glorious freedom of the children of God. We know that the whole creation has been groaning as in the pains of childbirth right up to the present time. Not only so, but we ourselves, who have the firstfruits of the Spirit, groan inwardly as we wait eagerly for our adoption as sons, the redemption of our bodies. For in this hope we were saved. But hope that is seen is no hope at all. Who hopes for what he already has? But if we hope for what we do not yet have, we wait for it patiently. (Rom 8:18–25)

This is a mystery: we cannot draw the lines demarcating where natural evil is an outworking of the freedom God ordained for all creation and where creation has been "subjected to frustration" by human malfeasance. Clearly much of the evil we experience is the consequence of human sin. But some suffering seems to be independent of human causality. All this occurs within the umbrella of the sovereignty of God.

When wrestling with the deepest questions of life, we must use something deeper than simplistic thinking. Some argue that if God is not in control of all, he is not in control at all. We must counter simple deduction with more complex reasoning based on observation of reality. At points, we must resign ourselves to the mysteries that are beyond our comprehension. While God is Lord of all, he is not the One who determines every detail of our existence. God gave us moral choice, and there are things that happen that are beyond the direct initiative of God.

Chapter 10

Other Angles on a Difficult Problem

The topic we are exploring is far too complex to be fully explained in the pages allotted here. Other resources are referenced for those who want to research some of the vast thought related to this discussion. In this chapter, we will touch on some of the remaining implications that follow a sound theodicy and some of the current alternatives: the soul-making theodicy of John Hick, process theology, and open theism. We will find insight from the pit of the Nazi concentration camp. We will briefly consider the implications for theodicy of the Christian belief in the miraculous and the afterlife.

God had to create a situation that would allow us freedom to make moral choices. If we knew God perfectly and understood the consequences of our choices, we would love God perfectly and would always do the right thing. John Hick says that we need an "epistemic distance" to be able to choose freely.[1] As Jesus said, blessed are they who have not seen..." We have to choose to trust God, even when we look through a dark glass. "God reveals Himself obscurely because He seeks to redeem us WITH our cooperation and not by means of tyranny. If God revealed Himself with earthly greatness, He would win us over in a worldly way. If there were no mystery—if clear as a bell

---

1. Hick, *Evil and the God of Love*, 379–80ff. Epistemology is the study of knowing: How do we know? So "epistemic distance" is a gap of ignorance.

intellectually—our intellect would assent but we would still be devoid of charity."[2] Since we do not fully understand the consequences of our decisions, we often make the wrong choice.

Some say that even if God allowed evil, a good God would never allow the magnitude of evil we experience. Often the first case study mentioned is the horror of Auschwitz.[3] But if freedom is authentic, then God cannot restrict the degree to which we might choose evil. Vieth makes a good case that none of us are far from committing the horrors of Auschwitz.[4] A common assertion is that there must be enough good to counterbalance evil for God to be just; but does this matter if the issue is freedom? Michael Peterson says, "Among the possibilities open to man is that of freely choosing to bring about an utterly gratuitous evil."[5]

A very different approach to theodicy has been offered to the tradition built on Augustine. John Hick suggests that we can build this alternative on the writing of another church father, Irenaeus.[6] Irenaeus differentiated between the image of God in which we were created and the likeness of God that is our goal.[7] Where Augustine saw Adam as one created in innocence whose fall brought all of us into depravity, Irenaeus saw God creating man in a fallen state with a challenge to grow into godliness. "Irenaeus suggests than man was created as an imperfect, immature creature who was to undergo moral development and growth and finally be brought to final perfection intended for him by his Maker."[8] "Instead of

---

2. This thought was shared with me by my colleague Dr. Dennis Plies, who believes he may have gotten it from Tom Skinner.

3. The Holocaust was not the first example of genocide. Hitler referred to worldwide apathy concerning the slaughter of Armenians by the Turks. Then there is the travesty committed by Stalin. We have our own shame in reference to the Native Americans and to African Americans (Schilling, *God and Human Anguish*, 19–22).

4. Vieth, *Holy Power, Human Pain*, 59–109.

5. Peterson, *Evil and the Christian God*, 103.

6. I find similar thinking in the writing of Tertullian.

7. Hick, *Evil and the God of Love*, 211ff.

8. Ibid., 214.

the Augustinian view of life's trials as a divine punishment for Adam's sin, Irenaeus sees our world of mingled good and evil as a divinely appointed environment for man's development towards the perfection that represents the fulfillment of God's good purpose for him."[9] Hick asserts that the Augustinian scenario is not so much the message of Genesis 3 but is an interpretation developed by the apostle Paul.[10] In the perspective proffered by John Hick, sin is seen as a failure to live up to the potential God intends for us.[11] Hick fully assigns to God responsibility for willing evil. Hick also questions whether hell is eternal.[12] Hick's alternative can be summed up in this statement, "There are, then, two attitudes to evil within the Bible, one based upon the dualistic view of evil as the irreconcilable enemy of God and man, and the other upon a profound sense of the sole ultimate sovereignty and responsibility of God."[13] Some are finding this "soul-making" theodicy preferable to the moral choice theodicy.

In recent years, many theologians have found in the process philosophy of Charles Hartshorne, John B. Cobb, and David R. Griffin a framework for rethinking theology, including the issue of theodicy.[14] Process theology provides a radically different way of thinking about God than that offered by classic philosophers in the tradition of Aristotle and Aquinas. Process theology defines reality as a series of events in place of the traditional definition involving material substances. The God of process theology is both objective and subjective, in contrast with the classic philosophical concept of the immutability and impassibility of God. That is to say, this concept of God has room for God to interact with

---

9. Ibid., 215.
10. Ibid., 283.
11. Ibid., 262–65.
12. Ibid., 345–49.
13. Ibid., 357.
14. For a primer on process theology, see Mesle, *Process Theology*. John B. Cobb wrote a final chapter in response.

creation with compassion. Where Christian doctrine has long held that God created all things *ex nihilo*, process theology suggests God created the universe out of a pre-existing matter. Process theology emphasizes the interaction of people and things in a manner that nothing is predetermined. One of the most attractive concepts in process theology is that the God of process does not coerce but only works to persuade. Process theology moves us from theodicy to anthropodicy (righteousness of humanity or why do we allow evil?).[15] There is much about process theology that is appealing and may help overcome some of the difficulties of classic Christian theology.

Some hope to find a better path in the theology of open theism.[16] This promises much of the advantages of process theology without some of the difficulties. Where process theology tends to be popular among more liberal theologians, open theism appeals to more conservative scholars who want to conform to biblical revelation. Clearly we need a theology that is informed as much by biblical record as by Greek philosophy. Open theism offers a God who existed before the creation of humanity and who can choose to intervene (or coerce) at his discretion. The God of open theism shares power with his creation as a matter of loving choice.[17] Both process theology and open theism reject the concept of determinism, the idea that everything that happens is the result of God's decision.

Most disconcerting is the tendency among process theologians and open theists to deny that God knows the future.[18] The argument usually goes that it is nonsense to insist that God knows the future, as the future has not yet happened. How can God know what has yet to be decided by free creatures? This effort to respect

---

15. Instead of "the justice of God," the issue becomes "the justice of man." How can we do such things?

16. For a primer on open theism, see Pinnock, *Openness of God*.

17. Rice, "Biblical Support for a New Position," 15–16.

18. Millard J. Erickson discusses this at length in *What Does God Know and When Does He Know It?*.

the freedom of autonomous creation is laudable, yet this position fails to comprehend that God is not bound by time.[19] Time is a part of God's creation. God dwells in the dimension of eternity. He is yesterday, today, and tomorrow simultaneously. There is no before or after with God.[20] God has foreknowledge of all that will happen—but this foreknowledge does not predetermine our choices. As discussed earlier, God is not limited by the fact that he cannot rewrite history. There is no reason to reject God's foreknowledge in the name of freedom.[21]

We need to rethink our interpretation of Genesis 3. Much of Augustinian theodicy is built on a particular view of the fall of man. John Hick offers an interpretation of Genesis 1–2 that man was created with a fallen nature so that he would have to find his way to God consciousness.[22] Hick sees the story of the fall as mythological, seen as history in less sophisticated times.[23] Without necessarily agreeing with the theodicy of John Hick, we need to understand correctly the literary nature of the first few chapters of Genesis. What we have there is not so much historical narrative, as we would find in an encyclopedia, but a saga. This is a grand description of the truth that all things are created by God. Within the saga is the

---

19. "Integral to the question of divine power is the relation of God to time...For Him there can be no before or after. Events experienced by human beings as past, present, and future as grasped by God in one eternal now" (Schilling, *God and Human Anguish*, 237). Schilling does not support this view, going on to say "There is little empirical basis for such a view." He is moving against the weaknesses of the doctrine of immutability. But why reject eternity entirely?

20. The same insight applies to discussion of life after death. Some debate as to whether we pass directly to judgment or wait in some sort of purgatory or "soul sleep." But if the afterlife is a matter of eternity, then there is no before or after. When I die, I will be present with my saintly grandmother and my unborn descendents with no sense of chronological order.

21. Obviously, this use of foreknowledge does not connote predestination. Some would argue that the idea of God as timeless cannot be divorced from the ideas of God never changing (immutability) or never being moved (impassibility) (Erickson, *What Does God Know*, 138ff).

22. Hick, *Evil and the God of Love*, 373–74.

23. Ibid., 245–49.

depiction of humans misusing their choice to their own detriment. Does it really matter whether there was a historical person named Adam to whom Eve gave a forbidden fruit? One does not have to disown biblical authority to understand the use of metaphorical language. The point is that we all make choices that are contrary to God's best for us. The consequences of these choices are destructive. The fall depicted in this story is a universal reality in which we all have participated. It has been this way from the beginning of time. Let us not get hung up on being blamed for what Adam did. We are each guilty of sin. Each of us has joined in on the crime.

Why is it that so many are convinced that there is a reason for everything that happens? As we have discussed, one factor that drives this conviction is the logical deduction of the assumption that God is sovereign over everything. But there is also an experiential reason for this conviction. We yearn for there to be a reason so that our suffering will have some meaning. Victor Frankl wrote an important work on this subject after experiencing the horrors of a Nazi prison. Frankl says, "Suffering ceases to be suffering in some way at the moment it finds a meaning, such as the meaning of a sacrifice."[24] The key is that meaning is ascribed by the individual—it is not inherent to the experience. So some people insist that God made something happen whether or not God did. What Frankl discusses as "meaning" is actually "value." For example, he discusses a woman living a life that has worth.[25] Frankl rejects what he calls "pan-determinism."[26] Frankl insists that people have choice and are never determined by conditions. For example, in describing the concentration camps, Frankl notes the way some behaved as animals while others were noble.[27] As Frankl discusses so well, life is often too painful to believe that there is

---

24. Frankl, *Man's Search for Meaning*, 179.
25. Ibid., 184–87.
26. Ibid., 206–10.
27. Ibid., 213.

no explanation to be found to our sufferings. So we find solace in imagining that there is a reason, even when the implications are that God is a cruel ogre who doles out suffering on his children. I am arguing that we need to face up to a more sober reality: some things happen for no good reason.

One problem for the approach to theodicy taken here is the miraculous. The record of the Bible and the testimony of many people is that God does intervene at times. This runs counter to the conviction that the things that we experience cannot always be attributed to the direct hand of God. To say that everything that happens is not the will of God or the result of God's decision is not to say that God never takes action in history. If God does intervene, then the problem of justice seems to be compounded.[28] There are surely times when God directly rewards virtue or punishes sin. There are times when God contravenes the natural order by his own power.[29] But we should be slow to draw the conclusion that something that has happened to us is by God's design. More likely, we have experienced another of the happenstances of reality.

Some find a significant part of the answer in the promise of an afterlife: Whatever injustice we experience here, God will make it all right in the age to come. John Hick asserts that the promise of an afterlife is indispensable to a Christian theodicy.[30] In a time of growing disbelief, many continue to believe in a heaven and hell as depicted in the Bible. This does not require a direct relationship between the hardships we face here and our eternal reward. Such an expectation implies that God is more directly involved in the equation than seems to be the case. Those who accept God's

---

28. Gregory Boyd discusses the problems raised by the fact that God does intervene at times (Boyd, *Is God to Blame?*, 108–11). Schilling concludes his book with a discussion of the providence of God within the constraints of reality (Schilling, *God and Human Anguish*, 261–79).

29. "The notion that there are compelling scientific and philosophical arguments against the possibility of such divine actions is an Enlightenment myth we need to rid ourselves of" (Hasker, "Adequate God," 230).

30. Hick, *Evil and the God of Love*, 337–41.

gracious offer will enjoy eternity in his presence. Those who do not respond in faith will suffer everlasting separation. One can well question whether the bliss of heaven is a satisfactory payback for the horrors of Auschwitz or agonies experienced by countless others, but this does not matter, since it was not God who brought these terrible things about. Rather, the eschatological dimension brings a balance to the injustices of life in a cosmic sense: God is not mocked; his sovereignty is real; all creation will respond in submission to his authority eventually. But for now, life is chaotic.

Some will be dissatisfied with such an untidy explanation, but it seems that life is not that easy to explain. Much of what happens to us makes no sense at all. There is no reason why it happened. We live in a world where some things happen for no good reason. And this is a beautiful thing. God is not standing behind every event manipulating everything for his purpose. His purpose is that we participate in the grand design to engage in an authentic relationship with each other and with him. Stackhouse underlines that it is not freedom that is the issue but love. God granted us freedom, not for its own sake, but as a means to express his love for us and so that we could truly respond in love to him. "God, to put it bluntly, calculated the 'cost-benefit ratio' and deems the cost of evil to be worth the benefit of loving and enjoying the love of these human beings."[31] Moral choice is a temporary provision through which we have the decision to love God; eventually God will bring judgment.[32] We are left with an unending array of choices to make in the meantime. We have no one to blame for the consequences of our choices but ourselves. Even when we do the right thing, the outcomes are often less than we desired. Still, we must endure and make the most of the challenges presented. Such is the reality of surviving the tragedies of life.

31. Stackhouse, *Can God Be Trusted?*, 74.
32. Ibid., 80–81.

More Reading on Theodicy

Boyd, Gregory. *Is God to Blame?* Downers Grove, IL: Inter-Varsity, 2003.

Hick, John. *Evil and the God of Love.* New York: Harper & Row, 1978.

Oden, Thomas. *Pastoral Theology: Essential of Ministry.* San Francisco: Harper and Row, 1982. See the chapter titled "A Theodicy for Pastoral Practice."

Stackhouse, John Gordon. *Can God Be Trusted?: Faith and the Challenge of Evil.* New York: Oxford University Press, 1998.

Surin, Kenneth. *Theology and the Problem of Evil.* Eugene, OR: Wipf & Stock, 1986.

Vieth, Richard F. *Holy Power, Human Pain.* Bloomington, IN: Meyer-Stone Books, 1988.

Yancey, Philip. *Disappointment with God: Three Questions No One Asks Aloud.* Grand Rapids, MI: Zondervan, 1988.

Yancey, Philip. *Where Is God When It Hurts?* Grand Rapids, MI: Zondervan, 1977.

Young, William P. *The Shack.* Newbury Park, CA: Windblown Media, 2007.

Section 4

Going a Little Deeper

Chapter 11

Job Does Not Answer the Question

Conversations about the problem of suffering inevitably turn to the book of Job in the Bible. Many assume that Job was written to explain why a loving and all-powerful God allows bad things to happen. But Job was not written as a textbook on theodicy. Those who turn to Job to answer the Great Triadox either walk away frustrated or put answers in Job's mouth that he does not speak. What theodicy is found in Job is patently false. "One of the central points of this profound book is to expose the shallowness of this popular theology."[1] In this chapter, I hope to discuss Job to determine what it does offer for those facing the tragedies of life.

Perhaps the first issue for consideration is the nature of this piece of literature. Many presume that Job is an historical account. Some insist that it is imperative that we read the book this way. They even argue that one who denies the historicity of Job rejects the Bible entirely. One can believe that the Bible is the Word of God without thinking that it matters whether or not there ever was a person named Job. The assertion that Job must have been an historical character is rooted in a mindset that devalues fiction as a worthy medium for communicating deepest truths. Worthy fiction is found not only in the classic fairy tales but also in the most memorable teachings of Jesus, one of the world's greatest storytellers. Recognizing the book of Job as fiction does not demean

---

1. Boyd, *Is God to Blame?*, 89.

the Bible any more than Jesus saying, "A man was going down from Jerusalem to Jericho, when he fell into the hands of robbers" (Luke 10:30). The message of the book of Job is what matters, not its historicity. In the Hebrew Bible, Job is not grouped with the books of the Law nor with the historical narratives nor the Prophets. Job is a work of poetry and is part of the Wisdom Writings. This should tell us something. Job appears to have lived about the time of Abraham, and yet he is not presented as being a part of the chosen nation. This story was developed over generations to communicate profound truth about how a man of God faces the tragedies of life. As has so often been the case, the greatest truths are expressed in fictional stories.

As we read the book perceptively, we see clues in the way the details are presented that there are deeper issues than merely recounting a historical event. The person of Job is a classic literary character. The setting of the opening scene is beyond human history. The plot unfolds in classic storytelling style. An appreciation of the literary techniques used in Job does not devalue this great work of sacred literature but enhances it.

Job is not only the hero, Job is everyman. He is presented as one who had no flaws while elsewhere the Bible proclaims that no one (other than Jesus) is perfect (Prov 20:9; John 8:7; Rom 3:10, 23; 1 John 1:8). The point of this assertion of Job's blamelessness is to make the point that virtue and good fortune are not directly connected. This character is complex, yet this does not prove that he was a historical personage.

The first two chapters present a scene that the writer could not have witnessed. How does the writer know all the details that are listed in this narrative? He certainly did not observe the conversation between God and Satan. The only defense for those who claim this is historical narrative is that God revealed to the writer things that happened beyond history. This theory assumes a mechanical dictation theory of biblical inspiration. What we have here is classic storytelling. The opening scene is a literary device to set up the story. It is unfortunate that some proof-text these verses to build a theology of suffering or a doctrine of Satan. Study of serious biblical scholarship will reveal that this Satan is not the devil of the New Testament. As Boyd says, "Since we are dealing with an epic poem, it is misguided to press this prologue for literal details about God's general relationship to Satan."[2]

The development of the plot is that of a great story more than that of historical record. Skillful literary technique can be found in the messages relayed to Job. Notice the repetition as Job's servants recount their stories, each wrapping up with "and I am the only one who has escaped to tell you" (Job 1:15, 16, 17, 18). Again we see classic storytelling technique. The second conversation between God and Satan makes it clear that the point of the story is the relationship between faith and circumstance. The prologue concludes with Job responding in holiness and faith. It is significant that the prologue shows the friends at their best moment: they sit in silence mourning Job's losses and discomfort. We would do well to learn from this. Let us not be as foolish as these friends in expounding "wisdom" about the reasons for suffering.

Too many Christians trivialize this classic piece of literature by seeking to mine it for answers to their questions. The Bible is more than a book filled with cryptic messages in hidden code. Yet truth is revealed in the book of Job for those with eyes to see.

The middle part of Job is a lengthy portrayal demonstrating how the truth can be distorted into absolute falsehoods. Most of what Job's friends say has some basis in fact. But the result is thirty-five chapters of error. Job provides a serious roadblock for those who hold to a simplistic view of inspiration. If every word of the Bible is written directly by God, then we have a confused God. A more mature view of biblical inspiration is needed to appreciate

---

2. Ibid., 86.

the beauty of this great work of holy literature. The middle section of Job presents these "righteous experts" expounding what is commonly believed to be the truth about suffering: Job must be facing the tragedies of life because he has done something to deserve it. Job's pleas of innocence only prove his guilt.

Who cannot identify with Job's pleas? He wonders what life is worth. "Why is life given to a man whose way is hidden, whom God has hedged in?...I have no peace, no quietness; I have no rest, but only turmoil" (Job 3:23, 26). "I despise my life; I would not live forever. Let me alone; my days have no meaning" (Job 7:16). Job wishes he had never been born. "Why then did you bring me out of the womb? I wish I had died before any eye saw me. If only I had never come into being, or had been carried straight from the womb to the grave!" (Job 10:18–19). Job despairs of finding God, saying "If I go to the east, he is not there; if I go to the west, I do not find him" (Job 23:8). Job wants his day in court asking, "Why does the Almighty not set times for judgment? Why must those who know him look in vain for such days?" (Job 24:1). "I cry out to you, O God, but you do not answer" (Job 30:20). Have you never been there? Job is everyman.

Job's friends (the antagonists) offer nothing but words of torment. "Consider now: Who, being innocent, has ever perished? Where were the upright ever destroyed? As I have observed, those who plow evil and those who sow trouble reap it" (Job 4:7–8). "Job, everybody knows that life is fair. Everybody gets what they deserve." Job's friends keep needling him to "fess up," confident that there must be a reason why God has done all this. "Blessed is the man whom God corrects; so do not despise the discipline of the Almighty. For he wounds, but he also binds up; he injures, but his hands also heal" (Job 5:17–18). "Surely God does not reject a blameless man" (Job 8:20a). The friends suggest that Job's claims of innocence only prove his guilt. "Is it for your piety that he rebukes you and brings charges against you? Is not your wickedness great? Are not your sins endless?" (Job 22:4–5). With friends like these, who needs enemies? Sadly, the words of Job's friends are not unlike those of some Christians today. We must not seize on these lines from Job's friends to define God's answer to the questions of theodicy.

Out of all of this misery, Job manages to hold on to the core of his faith. "Though he slay me, yet will I hope in him" (Job 13:15a). "I know that my Redeemer lives, and that in the end he will stand upon the earth" (Job 19:25). I love the song that begins, "Blessed be your name." But the bridge takes from Job the words "You give and take away." I find this a sad distortion of God's Word. Yes, God is sovereign. But Job was speaking out of his despair when he spoke these words (Job 1:21). Job's devotion should be emulated, but we should not build a theodicy on the idea that it is all God's "giving and taking away." As argued elsewhere, God should not be blamed for our misfortunes.

When we finally get to chapter thirty-eight, God speaks. All this time, Job has been asking why God doesn't show up and explain all this. God finally does show up, but he doesn't explain anything. "The LORD said to Job: 'Will the one who contends with the Almighty correct him? Let him who accuses God answer him'" (Job 40:1–2). Instead of answering questions, God simply riddles Job with the mysteries of life. God does this not once, but twice. Job tries to respond with contrition, but God continues to chew him out: "You have questions for *me*? I have some questions for you. Sit down for a minute and see if you can explain these things. You think you know so much, where were you…" Stackhouse offers this interpretation, "It is one thing to grieve over one's own unhappiness; it is quite another thing to go on to pronounce judgment on God's administration of the world."[3]

---

3. Stackhouse, *Can God Be Trusted?*, 94.

Job shows his stuff in the way he responds to God's rebuke. All this time, Job has been protesting his innocence and demanding that God give him an audience. After God's first tirade, Job says, "I am unworthy—how can I reply to you? I put my hand over my mouth. I spoke once, but I have no answer—twice, but I will say no more" (Job 40:4–5). After God's second tirade, Job says, "I know that you can do all things; no plan of yours can be thwarted. You asked, 'Who is this that obscures my counsel without knowledge?' Surely I spoke of things I did not understand, things too wonderful for me to know. You said, 'Listen now, and I will speak; I will question you, and you shall answer me.' My ears had heard of you but now my eyes have seen you. Therefore I despise myself and repent in dust and ashes" (Job 42:2–6). Job finally gets it.

> Job stopped asking questions not because God was a bully but because Job finally beheld God's unfathomable greatness in his immediate experience. He had spoken about God; then he came to know God. On meeting the real God, he simply had no more questions to ask. He discovered that God is the answer to all his questions, even questions he had not thought to ask. Job learned that behind the apparent randomness of life is the existence of God, whose greatness transcended Job but did not nullify the importance of Job's choices. Job ultimately found meaning in the ineffable presence of God, which he could not fully comprehend with his intellect but could only experience in the depths of his being.[4]

These words from a contemporary Job ring in my soul with their truth.

The epilogue offers more clues that should inform us on proper interpretation of this book. After God has thoroughly reamed

---

4. Sittser, *Grace Disguised*, 102–3.

Job, he turns on the friends. To paraphrase, he says, "You pompous hypocrites." More directly, "You have not spoken of me what is right, as my servant Job has" (Job 42:7). God declares Job to be the righteous one who needs to intercede for these windbags. The epilogue wraps up with a classic happy ending. Those who get hung up on the historicity of the book puzzle over how any number of children and livestock can replace that which Job lost. This is missing the point. The point is that there is no direct connection between our righteousness and suffering. Job is a morality play. Perhaps we might better recognize this if the script began with "Once upon a time…" and ended with "and they all lived happily ever after."

Job does not answer the question. It does not prove that God exists; the existence of God is assumed to be a fact. It does not explain why bad things happen to us. Those who emphasize the prologue to say that God allows Satan to test us are abusing this beautiful piece of inspired literature to propound theological fine points that were never intended. We can learn from Job that "it rains on the just and the unjust."[5] We can learn that God doesn't have to answer any of our questions. We can learn that truth is often more complex that our simplistic deductions. We can learn how harmful believers can be with their well-intended "words of wisdom." We can learn that true faith holds on through doubt and devastation. We can learn that people of faith sometimes question God (although Job was chastised for this). But we will not learn from Job the explanation as to why God allows us to suffer. "Job passes his test not because his theology is correct but because he does not reject God *even when his theology tells him he should.* Despite his theological misconceptions and impious rantings, Job's heart remains honest with God."[6]

---

5. This is a loose paraphrase of Matthew 5:45.
6. Boyd, *Is God to Blame?*, 94-95.

Chapter 12

Indications of Determinism in the Bible

Discussion of the problem of theodicy inevitably leads to quotations from the Bible. A number of these verses are problematic, at least at first blush. A healthy view of suffering depends on a sophisticated approach to biblical interpretation. Without engaging in a comprehensive discussion of hermeneutics (the art of interpretation), some acknowledgement of basic principles related to specific scriptures that seem to fly in the face of the thesis of this book is required.

Some take a simplistic approach to understanding the Bible. The assumption is made, perhaps with apologetic defense, that the Bible is inspired by God. Logical deductions are made that because the Bible is inspired by God, there must be nothing in the Bible that is not true. After all, a holy God could not lie. Those who take such an approach usually marshal the word *inerrancy* as the nonnegotiable password. Because the Bible is inspired by God, it must be without error. If there were any contradictions found in the Bible, its authority would be irreparably damaged as the basis for faith and living.[1] Suffice it to say that this simplistic approach is not adequate to solving the problems of life. In fact, the doctrine of inerrancy sets up the Bible for easy refutation by the skeptic who finds the first documentable error.

---

1. I discuss this matter in my book *Are You Sure You're Right?*.

We need a more adequate approach to understanding the nature of the Bible. The Bible is the uniquely inspired Word of God. But careful study of the Bible reveals a complexity in the records found there. Some of the ideas found in the Bible seem terribly primitive and out of character with the God that is revealed elsewhere. We should not be surprised at such diversity of views in a book written by multiple authors over a number of centuries. While God inspired all of the writers of Scripture, he had to work within the limits of their understandings and worldviews. This hermeneutic of accommodation recognizes that in revealing truth, God cannot exceed our ability to comprehend. Were God to reveal Scripture today, surely he would speak in terms of quantum physics and abstract math. We cannot expect the intricate nuances of modern culture to be expressed in literature that was composed by ancient writers. Instead, what we find in the Bible is a progressive revelation that evolves from the earliest books of the Old Testament to the relative maturity found in the New Testament. All of this is the Word of God, but we must use care in transposing these revelations to contemporary applications.[2] Even now, our minds are surely unable to comprehend all of the glory of God. We must be prepared to find statements in the Bible that fall short of adequately explaining the complexities of life.

Samson is an Old Testament hero (Judges 13–17) that provides a metaphor for describing the paradox of divine inspiration and human authorship of the Bible. Samson was uniquely anointed by God from before birth. Samson was filled with the spirit of God, yet was fatally flawed. Samson was a deliverer raised up by God, yet was given to fits of rage and petty vengeance. With unflinching honesty, the writer of Judges tells us that this holy

---

2. For an in-depth discussion, see Rogers, *Biblical Authority*, or Rogers and McKim, *The Authority and Interpretation of the Bible*.

man consorted with a prostitute and engaged in other behavior unworthy of a role model. If such a one could be a man of God, then why must the Word of God be inerrant? The paradox of Scripture is that this piece of human literature truly is the Word of God. Some deduce that Scripture's identity as the Word of God prohibits any error, contradiction, or variant point of view. Truly, the integrity of the Bible as Holy Scripture shines through the diversity and foibles of its writers and characters.

The best way to address the many biblical texts that seem to contradict the thesis of this book is to list them. Others may use these to invalidate the authority of Scripture. We will engage these difficult texts with a high view of Scripture, believing that the Bible is the inspired Word of God. Still, some parts of the Bible are not easy to understand.

One of the beliefs of those who accept the idea of determinism is that God chooses who will be saved. This is often described as election or predestination. While there are many other verses that are used to support such a doctrine, it must be admitted that some verses, at least on face value, seem to indicate that God decides who goes to heaven. For example, the book of Acts tells of an effective evangelistic outreach during the first of Paul's missionary journeys. Following the sermon, we read, "When the Gentiles heard this, they were glad and honored the word of the Lord; and all who were appointed for eternal life believed" (Acts 13:48). The most direct interpretation of this verse clearly connotes that God appoints who will be saved. To counter this requires more discussion than is appropriate to the purpose of this book. Rather, we will simply recognize this verse and advise that there are alternative views on salvation that have been held by Christians for centuries.

There is no getting around the fact that the Bible indicates that there are times when God does intervene in history. One can accept this possibility without refuting the thesis that God does not direct everything that happens. The story of the Old Testament is the story of God intervening on behalf of his chosen people. Early in the story, one of the sons of Israel (Joseph) is sent ahead to Egypt to provide for the salvation of the entire family. Joseph consoled his brothers when they learned of his identity, saying, "Do not be distressed and do not be angry with yourselves for selling me here, because it was to save lives that God sent me ahead of you" (Gen 45:5); "It was not you who sent me here, but God. He made me father to Pharaoh, lord of his entire household and ruler of all Egypt" (Gen 45:8); and "You intended to harm me, but God intended it for good to accomplish what is now being done, the saving of many lives" (Gen 50:20). Earlier, Joseph declares that God had ordained the famine that fell on Egypt (Gen 41:32). One might quibble that this was the view of Joseph without acknowledging the truthfulness of the viewpoint. Or one might recognize this as a unique example applicable to the salvation history of the nation of Israel and not applicable to all people at any time. Or one could accept that God intervened in history on these occasions to further his plan for a chosen people.

The writer of Exodus certainly believed that God determined things. God influenced the birthrates among the slaves in Egypt (Ex 1:20–21). God moved powerfully upon Moses, almost forcing him into his calling (Ex 4:11-5:22). This conversation inevitably includes the verses that speak of God's hardening the heart of Pharaoh (Ex 7:3; 8:15; 9:12; 10:1, 20, 27; 11:3; 12:36; 14:4). We will discuss this later. God directed the ten plagues against Egypt forcing them to let his people go (Ex 10:4, 12–13, 14; 13:8). On other occasions, the idea that all things that happen are directed by God is expressed in the book of Exodus (21:13; 23:25–26, 30; 32:14). One response to all this is to acknowledge that this was the viewpoint of this primitive writer and to assert that later biblical revelation shows a more sophisticated understanding.

Elsewhere in the Old Testament, one can also find this assertion that God intervened in history to aid or chastise his people. Of Samson, we read, "His parents did not know that this was from the LORD, who was seeking an occasion to confront the Philistines; for at that time they were ruling over Israel" (Judg 14:4). After the story of Gideon, we have the report that God brought action against one of his sons and his supporters for a palace coup. "God sent an evil spirit between Abimelech and the citizens of Shechem, who acted treacherously against Abimelech. God did this in order that the crime against Jerub-Baal's seventy sons, the shedding of their blood, might be avenged on their brother Abimelech and on the citizens of Shechem, who had helped him murder his brothers" (Judg 9:23–24). The prophet Jeremiah offered these thoughts observing the consequences of disobedience that produced the exile.

> Her foes have become her masters;
>> her enemies are at ease.
> The LORD has brought her grief
>> because of her many sins.
> Her children have gone into exile,
>> captive before the foe.
>> (Lam 1:5)

> The LORD himself has scattered them;
>> he no longer watches over them.
> The priests are shown no honor,
>> the elders no favor.
>> (Lam 4:16)

> unless you have utterly rejected us
>> and are angry with us beyond measure.
>> (Lam 5:22)

Again, one can accept that God moved in unique ways on behalf of the nation of Israel without asserting that everything that happens is God's will.

Much more problematic are several verses that baldly assert that evil comes from God. The writers of Proverbs certainly indicate a deterministic view.

> Commit to the LORD whatever you do,
>> and your plans will succeed.
> The LORD works out everything for his own ends—
>> even the wicked for a day of disaster.
> (Prov 16:3–4)

> The king's heart is in the hand of the LORD;
>> he directs it like a watercourse wherever he pleases.
> (Prov 21:1)

One should be careful about building doctrines on the book of Proverbs. These are statements of wisdom that tend to be true, but they should not be interpreted as foolproof maxims from the mouth of God. More difficult are such sayings from the prophets.

> I form the light and create darkness,
>> I bring prosperity and create disaster;
>> I, the LORD, do all these things.
> (Is 45:7)

> Who can speak and have it happen
>> if the LORD has not decreed it?
> Is it not from the mouth of the Most High
>> that both calamities and good things come?
> (Lam 3:37–38)

When a trumpet sounds in a city,
    do not the people tremble?
When disaster comes to a city,
    has not the LORD caused it?
    (Amos 3:6)

The determinism indicated in these verses cannot be denied. These verses need to be taken on balance with the whole of Scripture. As Walter C. Kaiser Jr. says in discussing the Isaiah text, "What we can be sure of, however, is the fact that God is never, ever, the originator and author of evil. It would be just plain contrary to his whole nature and being as consistently revealed in Scripture."[3]

The Bible indicates that God will intervene in human affairs with blessings and curses. Those who honor God's covenantal expectation will reap his favor, and those who rebel against God will suffer consequences. In the book of Deuteronomy, Moses summarized the previous books of the Pentateuch in a farewell sermon to the people of Israel. He concluded his words with a list of blessings and curses. "If you fully obey the LORD your God and carefully follow all his commands I give you today, the LORD your God will set you high above all the nations on earth. All these blessings will come upon you and accompany you if you obey the LORD your God" (Deut 28:1–2). The blessings listed include:

- Fertility in childbirth, crops, and livestock.

- Military engagements will result in victory.

- The nation would be prosperous and powerful.

---

3. Kaiser, *Hard Sayings of the Old Testament*, 196. Kaiser also discusses the Lamentations text on pages 206–9.

But wait. There is a catch. "However, if you do not obey the LORD your God and do not carefully follow all his commands and decrees I am giving you today, all these curses will come upon you and overtake you" (Deut 28:15).

- Curses would be urban and rural.
- The blight would affect their children, their crops, and their livestock.
- Diseases would ravage the land, including mental illnesses.
- Enemies would be victorious in battle, subjugating the people.
- Plans for marriage, homebuilding, and business would be thwarted.
- The nation would be a laughingstock before the world.

Moses continued with great detail all of the negative consequences that would follow if the people made God their enemy. Moses reiterates:

> See, I set before you today life and prosperity, death and destruction. For I command you today to love the LORD your God, to walk in his ways, and to keep his commands, decrees and laws; then you will live and increase, and the LORD your God will bless you in the land you are entering to possess.
>
> But if your heart turns away and you are not obedient, and if you are drawn away to bow down to other gods and worship them, I declare to you this day that you will certainly be destroyed. (Deut 30:15–18a)

One can accept biblical promises such as these without expecting that everything that happens in life is the result of God's direct decision.

Many verses (especially in the Old Testament) clearly indicate that God punishes sin or disciplines his people. When Israel wandered in the wilderness, "the LORD sent venomous snakes among them; they bit the people and many Israelites died" (Num 21:6). Moses is quoted as saying, "Know then in your heart that as a man disciplines his son, so the LORD your God disciplines you" (Deut 8:5). Moses advised the people that they should not take lightly the graciousness of God: "After the LORD your God has driven them out before you, do not say to yourself, 'The LORD has brought me here to take possession of this land because of my righteousness.' No, it is on account of the wickedness of these nations that the LORD is going to drive them out before you" (Deut 9:4). David recognized the hand of God at play in his victories and low points (2 Sam 6:12; 16:10). Elisha recognized the intervention of God on behalf of the political and military affairs of Israel (2 Kings 3:13). The message of the prophets included assertions that current affairs were the result of God's chastising Israel for its sin (Lam 3:39; Mal 1:3; 2:2, 9). In the New Testament book of Hebrews, this view is also expressed: "Endure hardship as discipline; God is treating you as sons. For what son is not disciplined by his father?" (Heb 12:7). Surely God intervenes in history on occasion. Some suffering is the discipline of God. But this is a far cry from ascribing all suffering to God's plan. And "discipline" surely has a richer connotation than punishment.

Several have discussed the phenomenon of God's hardening someone's heart. Does God determine that people make wrong choices? Most widely known are the several verses that declare that God hardened the heart of Pharaoh when Moses was demanding the release of the children of Israel (Ex 7:3; 8:15; 9:12; 10:1, 20, 27; 11:3; 12:36; 14:4). Another repeated case is the heart of Saul when he failed as the first king Israel, leading to the anointing of David (1 Sam 10:9; 16:14; 18:10; 19:9; 26:12). There we read of an evil spirit from God that entered the heart of the king. A simple interpretation of 2 Samuel 24:1 has God leading King David into temptation: "Again, the anger of the LORD burned against Israel, and he incited David against them, saying, 'Go and take a census of Israel and Judah.'" Later, the story reports that the wrath of God fell on the entire nation for David's indiscretion. "David was conscience-stricken after he had counted the fighting men, and he said to the LORD, "I have sinned greatly in what I have done. Now, O LORD, I beg you, take away the guilt of your servant. I have done a very foolish thing'" (2 Sam 24:10). In a parallel account, the chronicler softens the blow to blame Satan rather than God for tempting the king: "Satan rose up against Israel and incited David to take a census of Israel" (1 Chron 21:1). Lesser known examples are Sihon, king of Heshbon (Deut 2:30); the conquest of the Hivites (Josh 11:19–20); and the fall of Amaziah, king of Israel. (2 Chron 25:20). From the New Testament come these words of the apostle Paul: "Furthermore, since they did not think it worthwhile to retain the knowledge of God, he gave them over to a depraved mind, to do what ought not to be done" (Rom 1:28). More difficult is this New Testament reference: "Therefore God has mercy on whom he wants to have mercy, and he hardens whom he wants to harden" (Rom 9:18). This matter has been well discussed by theologians and scholars for the last two thousand years. For example, early church theologian Irenaeus wrote, "In the present time also, God, knowing the number of those who will not believe, since He foreknows all things, has given them over to unbelief."[4] A mainstream interpretation is that God simply moved these persons to do what they freely

---

4. Irenaeus, "Against Haeresies," book 4, chap 29, v 2, 502.

chose. We might simply recognize that determinism is found among the earliest biblical writers but that later revelation gives us a more complete understanding. Romans 9–11 is certainly a difficult passage to interpret for those who affirm free will.

Several Old Testament passages can be cited as proof that God brings bad situations on people. The book of Job, discussed in detail in chapter 11, concludes with this: "All his brothers and sisters and everyone who had known him before came and ate with him in his house. They comforted and consoled him over all the trouble the LORD had brought upon him" (Job 42:11). This could certainly be argued to be a statement of a primitive perspective and is not necessarily a sound basis for a theology of determinism. Biblical texts assert that God controls the fertility of at least some women: Leah, Rachel, the mother of Samson, Naomi, and Hannah. Does this provide proof that every pregnancy is a divinely ordained event? Are these unique cases in the salvation history of the chosen nation, or is such the understanding of primitive people recorded in the earliest parts of the Old Testament?

Gregory Boyd contrasts several verses that imply that anything God wills must take place with other verses that indicate that God's will can be resisted.[5] "He stands alone, and who can oppose him? He does whatever he pleases" (Job 23:13). "I know that you can do all things; no plan of yours can be thwarted" (Job 42:2). Should these be interpreted as God's truth or as Job's misguided understanding? Likewise, we should be careful about quotes from the Psalms. These are poetic statements drawn from hymns of faith: "Our God is in heaven; he does whatever pleases him" (Ps 115:3). "The LORD does whatever pleases him, in the heavens and on the earth, in the seas and all their depths" (Ps 135:6). Are these words authoritative as though spoken by

---

5. Boyd, *Is God to Blame?*, 177–78.

God himself or are they sincere exaltations of worship from well-intentioned people of faith? The book of Daniel records a similar assertion by Nebuchadnezzar after recovering from insanity. Bear in mind that these are the words of a nonbeliever (Dan 4:35–37). In contrast are verses indicating that God's will can be thwarted: "They rebelled and grieved his Holy Spirit. So he turned and became their enemy and he himself fought against them" (Is 63:10). "The Pharisees and experts in the law rejected God's purpose for themselves, because they had not been baptized by John" (Luke 7:30). Stephen said in his last sermon this indictment, "You stiff-necked people, with uncircumcised hearts and ears. You are just like your fathers: You always resist the Holy Spirit" (Acts 7:51). Paul cautioned the Ephesians, "Do not grieve the Holy Spirit of God, with whom you were sealed for the day of redemption" (Eph 4:30). Hebrews offers several warnings against apostasy:

> Do not harden your hearts as you did in the rebellion, during the time of testing in the desert. (Heb 3:8)

> We have come to share in Christ if we hold firmly till the end the confidence we had at first. (Heb 3:14)

> Therefore God again set a certain day, calling it Today, when a long time later he spoke through David, as was said before: "Today, if you hear his voice, do not harden your hearts." (Heb 4:7)

Does it matter that our texts indicating that God's will can be resisted are mostly from the New Testament, whereas we were listing verses from the Old Testament indicating a more deterministic view? If the concept of progressive revelation has any credence, it seems the further we venture into the Bible, the more we find expressions of free will countering assertions that God determines all things.[6]

In his excellent book on theodicy, Gregory Boyd offers profound thinking on the doctrine of predestination. "God sometimes predestines events, but he doesn't predestine individuals."[7] In Acts, we have assertions that God predestined that Jesus face the crucifixion. "This man was handed over to you by God's set purpose and foreknowledge; and you, with the help of wicked men, put him to death by nailing him to the cross" (Acts 2:23). "Indeed Herod and Pontius Pilate met together with the Gentiles and the people of Israel in this city to conspire against your holy servant Jesus, whom you anointed. They did what your power and will had decided beforehand should happen" (Acts 4:27–28). We can take these statements at face value without extending predestination to the experience of all people.

To be frank, some of the biblical texts are difficult to comprehend. Second Kings 15:5 asserts that God struck righteous King Azariah with leprosy. Paul seems to declare that God will use deception to accomplish his will: "For this reason God sends them a powerful delusion so that they will believe the lie" (2 Thess 2:11). In the conversation between God and Moses, we have a verse that could be interpreted to imply that God creates disabilities. "Who gave man his mouth? Who makes him deaf or mute? Who gives him sight or makes him blind? Is it not I, the LORD?" (Ex 4:11). Was Judas predestined to betray Jesus or did he act out of free will? "Jesus had known from the beginning which of them did not believe and who would betray him" (John 6:64). "I am not referring to all of you; I know those I have chosen. But this is to fulfill the scripture: 'He who shares my bread has lifted up his heel against me'" (John 13:18). "While I was with them,

---

6. Boyd offers an excellent discussion about ancient thinking about sovereignty (Ibid., 90–91).

7. Ibid., 186.

I protected them and kept them safe by that name you gave me. None has been lost except the one doomed to destruction so that Scripture would be fulfilled" (John 17:12).

In contrast to these many verses that seem to teach that all things are determined by God, there are a few texts that expressly declare that God is never responsible for evil. "He is the Rock, his works are perfect, and all his ways are just. A faithful God who does no wrong, upright and just is he" (Deut 32:4). "Like water spilled on the ground, which cannot be recovered, so we must die. But God does not take away life; instead, he devises ways so that a banished person may not remain estranged from him" (2 Sam 14:14). "For he does not willingly bring affliction or grief to the children of men" (Lam 3:33). While I am working to address the verses that seem to conflict with my belief, the determinist must account for these words from the Bible.

If this answer is to be found in a simple balance sheet calculation, the Bible clearly proclaims that God decides all things, including the creation of evil. I engaged in this exercise as an act of integrity to acknowledge that the Bible does present verses that are problematic for the kind of theodicy I propose. As I have sought to demonstrate, some texts offer multiple possibilities for interpretation. A big-picture perspective considering the progressive nature of biblical revelation allows for consideration of the thornier texts. At times, one has to avoid making dogmatic assertions that seem to fly in the face of biblical revelation. But one also has to recognize the implications of laying all the evil of the world at the feet of God.

An intriguing alternative has been offered by Bart Ehrman.[8] Ehrman is a former fundamentalist who turned to atheism. Ehrman argues there are multiple theodicies to be found in the Bible. The "classical view" is that suffering is punishment for sin. This is

---

8. Ehrman, *God's Problem*.

the view of Deuteronomy and the prophets. A "redemptive view" is that suffering produces a greater good. The story of Joseph is one example. Others are found in the plagues on Egypt and the death of Jesus. Ehrman finds two views in Job: the narrative of the introduction and conclusion present one view and the poetic middle presents another. The narrative portions present suffering as a test to prove one's faith. The poetic portions argue that there is no rational reason for suffering. The idea of suffering as a test is also found in the story of Abraham and Isaac. Ecclesiastes echoes the argument that there is no way to explain evil. The apocalyptic literature (especially Daniel and Revelation) argues that suffering is the result of demonic powers at work in the world that will soon be overruled by God. Ehrman argues that Jesus and Paul also held apocalyptic theodicies. Ehrman shows a profound understanding of the different genres of Scripture. (He is, after all, a professor of New Testament.) He also writes as one whose theological journey has departed the Christian faith. For Ehrman, all that is left is a humanistic plea to make this world the best we can. This is an intellectually sound argument, but unacceptable to people who are convinced that God is real and that the Bible is the inspired Word of God.

Some will no doubt find parts of this chapter objectionable. As we have demonstrated, the Bible is complex in its consideration of the problem of theodicy. The easy course is to cite only those verses that support our preconceptions. If we take the Bible seriously as the Word of God, we must engage all that it reveals.

Chapter 13

Embracing the Pain

In this chapter, we will dig a little deeper into the process of embracing the pain so that we can find deliverance and healing. Our first response is to recoil from that which shatters our soul. Denial is a nearly universal response to grieving. But if we give in to this impulse, we will never overcome the tragedies of life. We will not find peace by repressing our pain. We must grab our pain by the horns and face that demon in the eyes. As Henry Nouwen says, "The first step to healing is not a step away from the pain, but a step toward it."[1]

Gerald Sittser offers a voice of experience, having lost his four year old daughter, his wife, and his mother in a head-on collision. Sittser shares deep wisdom saying, "The quickest way for anyone to reach the sun and the light of day is not to run west, chasing after the setting sun, but to head east, plunging into the darkness until one comes to the sunrise."[2] Reality runs contrary to what we often imagine to be the case. We want to ignore our pain. We hope that if we don't think about it, the pain will go away.

> Denial puts off what should be faced. People in denial refuse to see loss for what it is, something terrible that cannot be

---

1. Nouwen, *Life of the Beloved*, 94.
2. Sittser, *Grace Disguised*, 33.

reversed. They dodge pain rather than confront it. But their unwillingness to face pain comes at a price. Ultimately it diminishes the capacity of their souls to grow bigger in response to pain. They make the same mistake as the patients who, following major surgery, refuse to get out of bed and put damaged muscles back to work. They pretend nothing is wrong and tell everyone that they are feeling wonderful. But denial of their problem causes muscles to atrophy until they cannot get out of bed at all. In the end denial leads to a greater loss.[3]

If we want to be free from the pain of loss and suffering we must engage it head on. Are you prepared to walk, or will you lie forever by the pool waiting for healing? (John 5:1–11). As horrible as your circumstances have been, they can be the occasion of growth, if you will make that choice.

Emotions have to be felt. When we try to repress our emotions, we only damage ourselves. The only way to healing is to allow the emotions to be expressed in a healthy manner. As we do, we find that they lose their power.

> This depth of pain is the sign of a healthy soul, not a sick soul. It does not have to be morbid and fatalistic. It is not something to escape but something to embrace. Jesus said, "Blessed are they that mourn, for they will be comforted." Sorrow indicates that people who have suffered loss are living authentically in a world of misery, and it expresses the emotional anguish of people who feel pain for themselves or for others. Sorrow is noble and gracious. It enlarges the soul until the soul is capable of mourning and rejoicing simultaneously, of feeling the world's pain and hoping for the

---

3. Ibid., 47.

world's healing at the same time. However painful, sorrow is good for the soul.[4]

Loss is inevitably painful. The only way to avoid this pain is to never engage in love. But what kind of life would that be, to never love anyone or anything? "Only the dead feel no pain, and that includes dead people who, though still alive, have rejected love and goodness and sorrow for so long that they have lost the ability to feel anything."[5] Elizabeth and I made a wonderful trip to England in September 2012. We had a chance to do some family research and to see many of the famous sites of London. While exploring, we came upon a beautiful monument in Grosvenor Park to those who lost their lives in the terrorist attacks of September 11, 2001. Engraved over the top of the wooden shelter there is the phrase: "Grief is the price we pay for love." That is so true. The easiest way to avoid grief is to never have a relationship with anyone or anything that has any meaning. But that is too high a price to pay to avoid pain. As we enjoy the ecstasies of love, we set ourselves up for eventual loss and pain. That is the cycle of life. One way to reduce the pain of loss is to celebrate the joy of what we had. Reflect on and talk about the precious memories, and let the tears flow.

Part of embracing the pain is presenting that pain to God in prayer. Earlier, we discussed the idea of raging at God as a healthy part of coping with pain. The Bible is full of songs of lament—protests before God for the suffering of the psalmist. We are given this prayer from Moses: "Relent, O Lord. How long will it be? Have compassion" (Ps 90:13). The prophet Jeremiah raged at God, accusing God of engaging in deception by breaking his promise: "Then I said, 'Ah, Sovereign Lord, how completely you have deceived this

---

4. Ibid., 63.
5. Ibid., 45.

people and Jerusalem by saying, "You will have peace," when the sword is at our throats'" (Jer 4:10). Psalm 102 carries this ascription, "A prayer of an afflicted man. When he is faint and pours out his lament before the LORD." This lament begins,

> Hear my prayer, O LORD;
> > let my cry for help come to you.
> Do not hide your face from me
> > when I am in distress.
> Turn your ear to me;
> > when I call, answer me quickly.
> (Ps 102:1–2)

How many times have you felt that God was turning his back on you? The prayers of the psalmist provide a vehicle for raging at God, for voicing your own feelings of pain.

> Will the LORD reject forever?
> > Will he never show his favor again?
> Has his unfailing love vanished forever?
> > Has his promise failed for all time?
> Has God forgotten to be merciful?
> > Has he in anger withheld his compassion?"
> (Ps 77:7–9)

> How long, O LORD? Will you hide yourself forever?
> > How long will your wrath burn like fire?
> Remember how fleeting is my life.
> > For what futility you have created all men.
> (Ps 89:46–47)

No one knew better how to rage at God than David, the greatest king of Israel. When David lost his best friend to military action, he composed of song of lament that he taught his companions to sing: "How the mighty have fallen in battle. Jonathan lies slain on your heights. I grieve for you, Jonathan my brother; you were very dear to me" (2 Sam 1:25–26a). Among the psalms of David are these:

How long, O LORD? Will you forget me forever?
　　How long will you hide your face from me?
How long must I wrestle with my thoughts
　　and every day have sorrow in my heart?
　　(Ps 13:1–2a)

My God, my God, why have you forsaken me?
　　Why are you so far from saving me,
　　so far from the words of my groaning?
O my God, I cry out by day, but you do not answer,
　　by night, and am not silent.
　　(Ps 22:1–2)

You are God my stronghold.
　　Why have you rejected me?
Why must I go about mourning,
　　oppressed by the enemy?
　　(Ps 43:2)

I am in pain and distress;
　　may your salvation, O God, protect me.
　　(Ps 69:29)

One section of one of the Psalms of David begins with words of praise, "In God we make our boast all day long, and we will praise your name forever" (44:8). Then there is a pause and the tone quickly turns to a lament.

You have rejected and humbled us…
You sold your people for a pittance,
    gaining nothing from their sale.
You have made us a reproach to our neighbors,
    the scorn and derision of those around us.
You have made us a byword among the nations;
    the peoples shake their heads at us.
My disgrace is before me all day long,
    and my face is covered with shame
at the taunts of those who reproach and revile me…
All this happened to us,
    though we had not forgotten you
    or been false to your covenant.
Our hearts had not turned back;
    our feet had not strayed from your path.
But you crushed us and made us a haunt for jackals
    and covered us over with deep darkness.
If we had forgotten the name of our God
    or spread out our hands to a foreign god,
would not God have discovered it,
    since he knows the secrets of the heart?
Yet for your sake we face death all day long;
    we are considered as sheep to be slaughtered.
Awake, O Lord. Why do you sleep?
    Rouse yourself. Do not reject us forever.
Why do you hide your face
    and forget our misery and oppression?
    (Ps 44:9, 12–16, 17–24)

The great king of Israel, the one God called "a man after my own heart" is raging at God. "What are you doing, God? Why have you sent us up the river? We don't deserve this."

We can learn much from a study of the biblical laments. These words of pain and protest teach us how to pray when we are in the pit of despondency. One way to embrace your pain is to pray these scriptures. Read through the laments and make the words your own. Feel free to compose your own laments as you tell God how you feel.

We need to enrich our concept of worship to include the practice of lament. Many view worship as merely an act of praise. We sing songs of joy expressing the best of what it is to be a child of God. But biblical worship includes words of protest as we question God about the tragedies of life. In the process of worship renewal, some are rediscovering this reality and are restoring contemplation and lament to practices of corporate worship.

While God allows us to vent our emotions freely, an understanding of reality may make it difficult to rage at God. When we believe that God owes us something, it is easy to be resentful when life is unkind. As one comprehends the principles we have been discussing, anger toward God becomes less appropriate. We may still feel anger, but the object of our anger moves from God to people, things, or life in general. What remains is the truth that we need to own our emotions. If you are feeling anger, there is no advantage in denying that fact. Embrace your pain. Give you emotions a voice. Talk with God about the reality of what you perceive. Even if you feel that God has done you wrong, God can handle that. God has very broad shoulders. And your relationship with God is strengthened as you are authentic in expressing your perceptions.

The movie *The Apostle* was released with great acclaim as a portrayal of a Christian minister. I found much of the movie disturbing. But one scene portrayed brilliantly the point we are now discussing. The protagonist is pacing in his bedroom shouting out, "God? This is Sonny." A neighbor calls to protest the noise. His mother responds, "Sometimes Sonny talks to God, and sometimes he yells." God invites us to rage at him when our hearts are broken.

There may be residual work that must be done related to your loss. While you may be tempted to avoid these responsibilities, your recovery will be hastened as you clean up whatever mess remains. There will likely be some pain, but the process will be healthy. You must embrace your pain and push forward into the darkness.

One path to healing is to join in community with others who are struggling with similar experiences. God designed us as social creatures. Healing is facilitated by interacting with others who care about us. If you are not doing so already, you should find such a group and work with them to recover from your injuries. If such a group does not already exist, you can surely find people who share your need for recovery. Invite them to work with you as you work through the principles we have been discussing. As you lean on each other, you will find increasing freedom to walk and run. The first six chapters of this book are designed to offer a curriculum for a small group of people to work together to overcome their experience of the tragedies of life. Take the lead in forming such a group for your own health and for the benefit of others who have shared in experiences like yours.

Chapter 14

Helping Someone through the Tragedies of Life

If you are not the one who is suffering at the moment, you do not have to look far to find someone who is. How can you be a support for them? We began this discussion in chapter five. Let's conclude with a discussion of how to be an encouragement to someone who is facing a difficult ordeal.

One of the most vital ministries you can offer is simple presence. Do not worry about "saying the right thing." Your words are not the thing that will bring healing: it is your caring presence that makes a difference. Be willing to sit in silence, if needed. Do not pressure them into conversation. Do not feel that you have to answer any question they might raise. You are there. That alone is a gift. Perhaps your best ministry will be hanging out together doing something that seems unrelated to their loss.

Above all, avoid the urge to say those things that sound spiritual but are truly hurtful and false. We have all heard these pious statements that are offered in consolation. I developed this list of "Stupid Things You Should Never Say" for one of my ministry classes. These comments are generally used with someone who is facing the death of a loved one but sometimes come up in other contexts.

- Be grateful for what you had.

- In the long run, you'll be a better person.

- God must have known you were a strong person.

- God only chooses the prettiest flowers for his heavenly garden.

- God needed another soprano for his choir.

- There must be a reason.

- Other people have it worse.

- It's been six months; you should be over it by now.

- Cheer up. Things could be worse.

A common element in these comments is the assumption that everything that happens is the result of God's will. Even if that were true, these comments offer little solace for those who are struggling. The thesis of this book is that God does not ordain every detail of what happens in our lives. These kinds of comments should be eliminated as representative of an inadequate theology and insensitive to the needs of a hurting person.

A common mistake is to compare someone else's suffering to our own. One of the worst things we can say is, "I know just how you feel." Such a statement belittles the significance of the struggle they are facing. While wanting to be helpful, we may stir up resentment or even rage with such a response. As Henri Nouwen suggests, it is better to recognize the uniqueness of a person's struggle than to assume a commonality: "Each human being suffers in a way no other human being suffers."[1] Instead of trying to prove that we have been there ourselves, we will probably be more helpful saying, "I can't imagine how much this hurts."

---

1. Nouwen, *Life of the Beloved*, 65.

We should not be paralyzed by a fear of saying the wrong thing. You do not have to be the expert on their struggle. Accept the fact that you really don't know how they feel. If they are facing death, they are in a place you have never been and cannot really comprehend.[2] Rather, you should assume their competence; they can find the answer if you listen. You must be comfortable with not knowing all of the answers. And be very careful that you do not transfer the focus from them and their pain to whatever pain in your life is triggered by their suffering. This is not about you.[3]

People who are facing the tragedies of life will often attribute their suffering to the hand of God. The thesis of this book runs contrary to popular theology. Do not fall into the trap of trying to correct their thinking. Perhaps you have found liberation understanding the reality of free will and the fact that life is not fair. You do well to keep your insights to yourself and offer to be a support on which they can lean. In time, you may earn the right to share with them an alternative perspective. But the loving path is to accept their perception.

When you are working to help someone through suffering, you are acting as a representative of Jesus Christ. Earlier, we referred to the poem about footprints in the sand. Often people cannot find Jesus in the haze of their suffering. In these moments, you may need to be Jesus for them. You may have to carry them until they can walk on their own. Your role is to listen until you can understand what their needs are. Let them do for themselves what they can do. Where they need assistance, you can gently respond.

At some point, you must recognize your own limitations and utilize the expertise of others. Everyone who seeks to help others must develop the skill of referral. There is only so much you can

---

2. Oden, *Pastoral Theology*, 301–2.
3. Thanks to my colleague Dr. John Fazio for these insights. Besides being a professor of developmental psychology, Fazio serves in the Trauma Intervention Program with persons facing the most severe of losses.

do to help. If you ignore this reality, you will probably do more harm than good. Part of your ministry is to recognize what their needs are and where they can find help. You can use the confidence they have developed in you to encourage them to seek help from others who can truly bring healing. This may be another volunteer, or it may be a professional. If they are hesitant to act on a simple referral, you may need to offer to go with them to meet with someone who can help them.

Ministry with the bereaved

How do we help a person who is coping with the loss of someone they love to death? Everything we have discussed in this chapter applies to this setting. Your first ministry is presence; other friends may be hard to find in these days. Be careful not to say too much or to add to their grief. Allow them to help themselves as much as they can. Be there to aid where needed.

Avoid the use of euphemisms when trying to help a person who is bereaved:. It does not really help to use expressions such as *passed away* or *left us* in place of saying, "She (or He) died." Sometimes these substitutions may be helpful, but generally, we need to speak plainly. The word is *die*. Using direct terms helps us to fully embrace the tragedies of life.

A common misconception is that people who are bereaved need to be cheered up. This can be counterproductive. As we discussed in the previous chapter, the path to healing lies in facing the pain, not in escaping it. Instead of steering them away from their pain, you must allow them to embrace it. You can help them embrace the pain by talking with them about it. Ask them questions or share your own memories of the deceased. This may well bring tears, but they will be blessed by the remembrances.

Be aware of the need for friendship long after the death. In the period leading up to and following the funeral, plenty of people are available to be of help. The difficult times can come six weeks or six months later when no one is calling or expressing concern. Expressions of concern may be especially appreciated when everyone else has moved on.

A particular form of bereavement is found in the case of miscarried pregnancy. The couple (or single mother) had been building a dream of a child to come, only to have those dreams bluntly dashed. While miscarriage is always painful, the loss of a first pregnancy raises fears of childlessness. Your support can be valuable as they move forward into a future that is different than anticipated.

Similar dynamics may be present for a woman (or couple) who has aborted a child. Feelings of guilt may continue years after the decision. Advocacy efforts to reduce or eliminate abortion tend to be hurtful to those who at some point have chosen to terminate a pregnancy. Regardless of your conviction on freedom of choice or right to life, persons who have chosen abortion need your love and compassion.

Ministry with the dying

A significant ministry is available in the time before death with the person who is dying. Some dread this ministry, but there are few times when you will have a greater opportunity to make a difference than when you are helping someone who is dying. People who are facing death tend to respond to love and support far more than before. They may experience isolation as others recoil in fear. Even the doctor may pull back. Unfortunately, medical people are often trained to view death as the enemy, as some kind of a personal failure. Death is a natural part of life. Those who are walking this path continue to need someone upon whom they can lean.

We should understand that every case of death brings different issues. Some are ready to go. Some are relieved that the long battle is almost over. Some are anxious about what death will be like or how they will respond. Some are filled with a sense of guilt over something they have done or did not do. Some will be in shock that the end is bearing down on them so quickly. As much as ever, your first responsibility is to listen. Do not assume that you know what they are thinking or feeling. Find out firsthand how they are responding to their hardship.

More than ever, talk is not as valuable as silence. Do not be afraid to spend long periods just sitting with them. Choose your words carefully. Perhaps the best words you can share are found in the Bible, especially if they have a Christian faith. Share appropriate scripture without commentary. There is probably no wisdom you can compose that will match a simple verse of God's Word. Ask them if there are scriptures you can read for them. Have a verse ready if needed. Let the power of God's Word stand on its own. A sermon is probably not going to be very helpful. Join them in meditating on the truth in silence.

As people approach death, they often need a confidant. In some Christian traditions, a spiritual director is a valued resource for personal growth, renewal, or recovery. Part of being Jesus for someone includes hearing confession. I was visiting one man in the last week of his life. I had always known this man to be a strong person, not given to emotional display. With tears, he informed me of a decision made years earlier in a previous marriage to abort a baby. After all these years and many accomplishments, he needed to be unburdened of this horrible secret that still brought him shame after a half century. My role was simply to hear his confession and remind him of the forgiveness offered by Jesus Christ.

For those who are not familiar with the practice of confession (also known as absolution or reconciliation), let's consider how it is done. When someone shares their heart with us, we are to listen with the heart of Jesus. We must be mindful of our own sinfulness and of the fact that new life is a gift from God. We should listen and not give instruction or correction. When we have heard their confession, our job is simply to proclaim the truth that they are forgiven in Jesus' name. It is not that we forgive them but that on God's behalf we speak the forgiveness that Jesus offers. You might lay hands on them or even anoint with oil. This is a long-standing symbol of God's presence. Of course, confession and absolution is a serious responsibility that requires the keeping of confidences. With rare exceptions, what is entrusted to you must be kept in trust. We can set people free from guilt and shame by pronouncing the good news of the gospel. You do not have to be an ordained pastor or priest to take confession; you have authority in Jesus' name.[4]

Ministry with the sick

Illness is an experience most of us face several times during out lives. We may be suffering because our body is fighting bacterial or viral infection. We may be recovering from an injury. Or we may be in the aftermath of a medical surgery. In any case, we are prone to feel "dis-ease" during these times of illness. We may be incapacitated to some level and generally do not feel well. During these times, the support of a compassionate person can bring some relief. Let's discuss the possibilities of helping someone who is sick.

The person who is sick is susceptible to feeling lowly. Yet the Bible indicates that when we show love to a sick person, we are ministering directly to God (Matt 25:36). In some cases, the person may be ill as a consequence of choices made. But compassion is appropriate whether or not the person's behavior contributed

---

4. For more on the discipline of confession, see Foster, *Celebration of Discipline*, 143–57. The concept of spiritual authority is well discussed in Lovelace, *Dynamics of Spiritual Life*, 133–44.

to their illness. People who are not feeling well are prone to reflect on their condition in ways that may be negative. Encouragement is needed to direct their thoughts in healthy ways.

Part of our ministry with the sick is to pray for their healing. "Is any one of you sick? He should call the elders of the church to pray over him and anoint him with oil in the name of the Lord" (James 5:14). Jesus linked prayers for healing with the proclamation of the kingdom of God as the core of our mission (Luke 10:9). The psalmist declares, "Praise the LORD, O my soul, and forget not all his benefits—who forgives all your sins and heals all your diseases" (Ps 103:2–3). When praying for the sick, the time-honored practice is to lay hands on them and to anoint them with a drop of olive oil representing the power of the Holy Spirit.

When visiting the sick in a hospital setting, we must be mindful of our role. As a minister of the gospel, you should not underestimate your significance as a member of the healing team. People who are hospitalized tend to be very receptive to a caring visitor. But you must be respectful of proper protocol and of the others who are working to help patients. Do not expect to be given personal information by hospital staff. Enter a hospital room carefully, knocking at the door. If the door is closed, it is better to check with the nursing station as they may be indisposed to visitors at the moment. You should be mindful of hygiene when visiting in a hospital. Wash your hands as you enter and use a breath mint. You may find that the patient is asleep. If so, it is usually best if you wait in silent prayer for a few minutes to see if they awake. Hospital calls should be kept brief as the patient probably is limited in their endurance. Never sit on the hospital bed with the patient. Doing so may cause them more discomfort than you know. Better to pull up whatever chair is available. Sitting is better than standing, as it creates an impression of a substantial visit even when you stay only ten or fifteen minutes. Sometimes, the conversation may be frivolous and joyful, while other times may require a more somber tone and silence. If a patient is unconscious, you do well to pray out loud in case they are able to hear. Be flexible in allowing nurses and orderlies to do their work. You should never be pushy with spiritual direction or evangelistic effort. First and foremost, your presence expresses God's love. Reading scripture is often appreciated and should be done with minimal commentary. At times, your ministry with family members is as significant as with the patient. You may even have opportunity to serve the doctor or other medical professionals. Some people find the hospital environment to be uncomfortable, but this can provide a welcome place for service to the suffering.

Ministry with the divorced

Those who are recovering from divorce have many of the same needs as those who are bereaved. The pain of loss may be compounded by a sense of guilt that they could have prevented the loss. Where death brings permanent separation, divorce results in loss of relationship with a person who remains alive and may still be in contact. This grieving process can be protracted as the healing is repeatedly disrupted like tearing a scab off of a wound. Feelings of guilt are often compounded with judgment from others. The Bible quotes God as saying, "I hate divorce" (Mal 2:16). But the same Bible presents a God of second chances and redemption: "I am making everything new" (Rev 21:5).

In many social contexts, divorce turns the individual into a pariah. They are seen by others as having failed in one of life's most significant commitments. They may not be welcome in circles where they had once participated. They probably have severed family relationships beyond their ex-spouse. They may face economic consequences from their divorce.

Your role in ministering with a person recovering from divorce is to convey the love and acceptance of God. Listen to their concerns, fears, and regrets. While divorce is never God's will, neither is it so great a sin that grace and spiritual vitality are not available. Encourage them to make sound choices today as they construct their future.

Ministry with persons with disabilities

For some, the tragedies of life involve losing the abilities most people possess or being born without those abilities. Persons who are "dis"abled face stigmatization by a society that demands that everyone fit the expectations of normalcy. Disabilities include sensory limitations, mobility limitation, and mental limitations. For some, the tragedies of life include living with one of these limitations. For others, it is raising children who have birth defects or who are injured. We will now consider some of the issues in trying to help someone with a disability.

A fundamental principle for loving people with a disability is to use "people-first" language.[5] Many speak of people with a disability in ways that dehumanize them. Words have power to shape reality. Labels should be avoided in favor of descriptive terms that affirm their personhood. No one *is* "handicapped" or "a retard." Rather, they are "a person with a disability" or "a child with retardation." Rather than thinking of a "birth defect," we do better to think of a "congenital disability." The table on the facing page contains a list of possibilities for people-first language. This may seem to be nitpicking over semantics, but it strikes at the root of the identity of the person with a disability.

---

5. I am indebted to Kathy Snow for opening my eyes to the issue of people-first language at a conference for persons with disabilities and their parents.

Examples of people-first language

Avoid	Use
in special ed	receives special ed services
a Downs child/mongoloid	has Downs syndrome
crippled	has an orthopedic disability
dwarf	is of short stature
mute	is nonverbal
crazy	has an emotional disability
afflicted with/a victim of	has…
normal/healthy	typical/non-disabled
handicapped parking	accessible parking

When trying to be helpful with a person with a disability, we should keep in mind the basic rights due to all people. We all deserve to be treated with respect and dignity. We all want to make choices for ourselves instead of being told by someone else what we have to do. We all want at least one friend who truly cares about us and is interested in our thoughts and feelings. We all want to be able to communicate and to have our thoughts and wants clearly understood. We all want to participate in society, to make some contribution, and to be compensated fairly for our work. A fascinating concept is described as "dignity of risk." We sometimes feel we must shelter a person with a disability from experiences for their own safety. But children need to ride roller-coasters and experience the other thrills of life. Dignity of risk gives a person with a disability permission to engage in activities that might be unsafe.

If we are to be helpful to people facing disability, we must change the way we think. Don't be sorry about a wheelchair: it gives freedom, not restraint. Do we believe the Declaration of Independence? All persons are created equal, even those who cannot see or hear or walk. The child with a disability does not have a "problem"; we do. Do not discuss what they cannot do; discuss what they can do. Get away from "personal tragedy" theory; change to "social oppression" theory. There are no victims. Try to get away from seeking government aid for every problem to emphasizing natural supports among the family and friends who love the individual. Understand that adults with retardation are not "eternal children" but are adults who generally have all the desires of adults, including a hunger for intimacy.

Ministry in trauma (fire, theft, accident, abuse)

For some, the tragedies of life include overcoming a traumatic event. One day we heard an unusual number of sirens and looked outside to find the house just up the street from our driveway consumed in fire. Every day, someone comes home to find that their home has been burglarized or they have otherwise been a victim of theft. Our phone went off after midnight one night to inform us that our daughter had just had a collision resulting in the destruction of our family automobile. Every day, people suffer abuse, whether rape or sexual molestation, verbal abuse, or exploitation. How might you be of service to a person who has experienced trauma?

When life has been abruptly shaken, it is helpful to have someone who provides a steady support. Your reliable presence may be the only constant they can find. Allow them freedom to express their emotions. Offer to assist them in processing what they need to do in response to this unexpected event. You cannot replace them in making decisions, but you can help them put the pieces together.

Ministry with the impoverished

We can apply these same principles in relating with people who experience economic poverty. We do not have to look far to find people whose experience of the tragedies of life involves a struggle to find enough to eat, a safe and warm place to sleep, and the basics of life. Let's consider some of the issues in helping those who are poor.

The classic theologian Thomas Aquinas suggested there are three degrees of poverty: ordinary poverty, acute poverty, and destitution.[6] Ordinary poverty includes people we might describe as the working poor. These people may have a place to live and probably have regular employment, but their income is routinely inadequate to meet their basic needs. People who work at minimum wage levels can only generate so much income: a second or third job may not be enough to pay the bills. Aquinas suggests that we must first act to make sure that their situation gets no worse than it is already (preventative remedies) and then work to make things better (curative remedies). Acute poverty describes the crisis cases in which people who are normally self-sufficient are now facing economic distress. Aquinas suggests that we must act to address the crisis (emergency relief). Destitution is the level of chronic and extreme poverty. This includes people who live on the street. Not all people facing poverty are the same: we must strive to understand the unique needs of each individual.

People who are poor deserve to be treated with dignity. We are to see them as representatives of Jesus Christ (Matt 25:35–36). We need to understand that their situation may be conditioned by forces beyond their own control. Regardless of the degree of choice that has led to their condition, all people deserve to have their privacy respected. We must also be careful that we do not dehumanize them by enabling them to avoid their own responsibility. Your role is to encourage, to assist them in making sound decisions, and to help when you have resources.

---

6. Oden, *Pastoral Theology*, 273.

Ministry in job loss

We tend to identify ourselves by our jobs, so losing a job is a painful attack on our sense of worth. In the best of times, some are unemployed, and in times of economic turmoil, the number of those unemployed rises. People who are recovering from the loss of a job and seeking a replacement need the support of those who care for them.

Focus on encouraging them to exercise initiative. The fourth of our key principles (You are solely responsible for the decisions you make today. Do something.) is applicable here as much as ever. Whether or not they are responsible for bringing about their loss of employment is largely irrelevant. What matters is the effort they mount to locate their next job. Their fate is in their hands. Yet people who are unemployed often struggle with motivation as their sense of self-worth is diminished. Your ministry of encouragement may make all the difference. Be patient with them as they vent their feelings of frustration. Help them remember their own value and ability.

———————•———————

You can provide a valuable resource to others if you will choose to be a sensitive minister to people facing the tragedies of life. This ministry can provide great satisfaction as you funnel the love of God to people in pain. The best way to develop the skills needed is to practice what you already know with the people who are already present in your life. Blessings on you as you share God's grace in practical ways.

Epilogue

"Meaningless. Meaningless."
    says the Teacher.
"Utterly meaningless.
    Everything is meaningless."
    (Eccl 1:2)

Nothing makes sense!
Everything is nonsense.
    I have seen it all—
    nothing makes sense!
    (Ecc 1:2 CEV)

While many turn to the book of Job to find answers to the question of theodicy, perhaps we do better to look to the book of Ecclesiastes. Maybe there is no meaning to be found in suffering. In the words of Jack Sanders, "Unlike the author of Job, who was deeply concerned with the issue of theodicy, Qoheleth (or Ecclesiastes) rejects the theodicy question and asserts rather that life is both unfathomable and unjust; we may as well, therefore, enjoy life as long as we are able."[1]

> There is something else meaningless that occurs on earth: righteous men who get what the wicked deserve, and wicked men who get what the righteous deserve. This too, I say, is

---

1. Sanders, "Wisdom, Theodicy, Death."

meaningless. So I commend the enjoyment of life, because nothing is better for a man under the sun than to eat and drink and be glad. Then joy will accompany him in his work all the days of the life God has given him under the sun.

When I applied my mind to know wisdom and to observe man's labor on earth—his eyes not seeing sleep day or night—then I saw all that God has done. No one can comprehend what goes on under the sun. Despite all his efforts to search it out, man cannot discover its meaning. Even if a wise man claims he knows, he cannot really comprehend it.

So I reflected on all this and concluded that the righteous and the wise and what they do are in God's hands, but no man knows whether love or hate awaits him. All share a common destiny—the righteous and the wicked, the good and the bad, the clean and the unclean, those who offer sacrifices and those who do not.

> As it is with the good man,
> so with the sinner;
> (Ecc 8:14–9:2a)

"I have seen something else under the sun: The race is not to the swift or the battle to the strong, nor does food come to the wise or wealth to the brilliant or favor to the learned; but time and chance happen to them all" (Ecc 9:11). The writer repeats himself: "'Meaningless. Meaningless.' says the Teacher. 'Everything is meaningless'" (Ecc 12:8). What are his final thoughts? All we can do is live in obedience to God. "Now all has been heard; here is the conclusion of the matter: Fear God and keep his commandments, for this is the whole duty of man. For God will bring every deed into judgment, including every hidden thing, whether it is good or evil" (Ecc 12:13–14). Life is not fair. If we expect everything that happens to make sense, we will only be frustrated. Still, we are accountable before God for our choices.

The object of classic theodicy is to justify God. But if evil is not God's will or God's doing, then classic theodicy is misguided. Evil is never God's will. When we ask, "Why does God allow these things to happen?" we are asking the wrong question. As difficult as the tests of life are, the alternative would be the complete loss of our freedom.

> The experience of gratuitous evil whether in ourselves or in others links us to other beings and evokes a sense of the precariousness of existence, a kind of threat or nothingness that is a given ingredient of our being in the world. This precariousness of being is part and parcel of what it means to be, and if we are to deal with the problem of suffering we have to begin by accepting the precariousness of existence, including the senselessness of at least some forms of suffering.[2]

If we are to be mature, we must accept the senselessness of much that we experience in life. We must proceed from this understanding to take responsibility for all that is within our control. We must also emulate the compassion of God and reach out with care for those who suffer the tragedies of life. When we ourselves are injured by the tragedies of life, we do well to receive the grace of God and the compassion of those who care about us.

Let's review the four basic principles discussed in section two. These are built on biblical teaching interacting with the hard side of life.

1. God is still on his throne. Remember that.

2. Life is not fair. Embrace it.

---

2. Long, "Suffering and Transcendence."

3. There are persons who care for you. Lean on them.

4. You are solely responsible for the decisions you make today. Do something.

How are you doing in applying these principles to your life? This is best practiced in community rather than as a self-help project. As the Bible says, "It is not good for the man to be alone" (Gen 2:18). If you have not done so already, join with one or more persons who have similar struggles with your own to support each other.

We went further in section three to explore the work of a number of Christian theologians. While popular Christian teaching offers the simplistic view that the sovereign God makes everything happen the way it does, careful analysis offers a more complex perspective. Even with these insights, the tragedies of life are difficult to understand. Explanations from thoughtful people will be found to be inadequate. At points, we must simply choose to trust God in the face of life's mysteries. Our own concept of God may need to be refined as we reconcile his holiness with his love. The beauty is that no matter how badly we misconstrue his nature, God's love remains available to us. The key to thriving in life is to appreciate the freedom that God has given us. We truly are sons and daughters of the Almighty. We share with God responsibility for the past, the present, and the future. Victory in overcoming the tragedies of life depends on taking hold of our freedom and responsibility to make our decisions and actions in conformity to God's guidance. We need to use the resources that are made available to us through prayer. In soberness, we must avoid the deceptions that we can easily imagine that will only detract us from facing the realities of life.

As discussed in section four, our interpretation of the Bible can help or hinder our understanding of life. We need to read Scripture in a way that fits reality and the complexities of the record itself. This book was written with an assumption that the

Bible is the uniquely inspired Word of God. Since God revealed himself in literature, we must use literary analysis to mine all of the treasures there.

We concluded our discussion with practical applications. In a sense, this book is the result of fifty years of my life, or at least fifteen years of parenting and grieving. But all that I have written is pointless unless you choose to take appropriate action. First, you must decide to respond constructively to your own experience of the tragedies of life. No one can do that for you; all we can do is offer love and support. As you work to overcome your own challenges, I invite you to join God's team in ministering the love of God to others who suffer. This may be the best way to find joy in the midst of life's sorrows. Thank you for allowing me this privilege.

Bibliography

Aquinas, Thomas. *Summa Theologica*. Benziger Brothers edition, 1947.

Arthur, Kay. *When Bad Things Happen*. Colorado Springs, CO: Waterbooks Press, 2002.

Augustine. *Augustine: Confessions and Enchiridion*. Translated by Albert C. Outler. Philadelphia: Westminster Press, 1955.

Biebel, David B. *If God Is So Good, Why Do I Hurt So Bad?* Colorado Springs, CO: Navpress, 1989.

Boethius, *The Consolation of Philosophy*, Book 1. http://etext. virginia.edu/latin/boethius/boephil.html (accessed June 25, 2008).

Boyd, Gregory. *Is God to Blame?* Downers Grove, IL: InterVarsity, 2003.

Christian Century. "Where Was God? An Interview with David Bentley Hart." *Christian Century* 123, no. 1 (January 10, 2006): 26–29

Davis, John Jefferson. "The Holocaust and the Problem of Theodicy: An Evangelical Perspective." *Evangelical Review of Theology* 29, no. 1 (January 2005): 52–76. ATLA Religion Database.

Dobson, James, Jr. *When God Doesn't Make Sense*. Carol Stream, IL: Living Books, 2001.

Ehrman, Bart D. *God's Problem: How the Bible Fails to Answer Our Most Important Question—Why We Suffer*. New York: HarperOne, 2008.

Erickson, Millard J. *What Does God Know and When Does He Know It?* Grand Rapids, MI: Zondervan, 2003.

Flew, Anthony. "Divine Omnipotence and Human Freedom." In *New Essays in Philosophical Theology*, edited by Anthony Flew and Alasdair MacIntyre. New York: MacMillan, 1963.

Foster, Richard J. *Celebration of Discipline.* 20th anniversary ed. San Francisco: HarperSanFrancisco, 1998.

———. *Prayer: Finding the Heart's True Home.* New York: HarperOne. 1992.

Frankl, Viktor. *Man's Search for Meaning.* New York: Washington Square Press, 1963.

Hasker, William. "An Adequate God." In *Searching for an Adequate God : A Dialogue between Process and Free Will Theists,* edited by John B. Cobb and Clark Pinnock, 215–45. Grand Rapids, MI: Eerdmans, 2000.

Hauerwas, Stanley. *Naming the Silences: God, Medicine, and the Problem of Suffering.* Grand Rapids, MI: Eerdmans, 1990.

Hick, John. *Evil and the God of Love.* New York: Harper & Row, 1978.

Hickson, Jerry A. *Are You Sure You're Right?* Anderson, IN: Warner Press, 2006.

Hume, David. *Dialogues Concerning Natural Religion.* New York: Social Science Publishers, 1948.

Irenaeus. "Against Haeresies." In *The Ante-Nicene Fathers: Translations of the Writing of the Fathers down to A.D. 325,* edited by Alexander Roberts and James Donaldson. Peabody, MA: Hendrickson Publishers, 1995.

Kaiser, Walter C., Jr. *Hard Sayings of the Old Testament.* Downers Grove, IL: InterVarsity Press, 1988.

Kreeft, Peter. *Making Sense Out of Suffering*. Ann Arbor, MI: Servant Books, 1986.

Kushner, Rabbi Harold. *When Bad Things Happen to Good People*. New York: Anchor Books, 2004.

Lewis, C. S. *The Problem of Pain*. New York: Harper, 1942.

Long, Eugene Thomas. "Suffering and Transcendence." *International Journal for Philosophy of Religion* 60, no. 1–3 (December 2006): 139–48. ATLA Religion Database.

Lovelace, Richard. *Dynamics of Spiritual Life: An Evangelical Theology of Renewal*. Downers Grove, IL: InterVarsity Press, 1979.

McLaren, Brian D. *The Secret Message of Jesus: Uncovering the Truth That Could Change Everything*. Nashville, TN: W Publishing Group, 2006.

Mesle, C. Robert. *Process Theology: A Basic Introduction*. St. Louis: Chalice Press, 1993.

Moltmann, Jürgen. *The Crucified God*. Translated by R. A. Wilson and John Bowden. New York: Harper, 1974.

Neibuhr, H. Richard. *The Responsible Ethic*. New York: Harper and Row, 1963.

Nouwen, Henri J. M. *Life of the Beloved*. New York: Crossroad, 1992.

———. *The Way of the Heart: Desert Spirituality in Contemporary Ministry*. New York: HarperOne, 1991.

Oden, Thomas. *Pastoral Theology*. Nashville, TN: Abingdon, 1983.

Peterson, Michael. *Evil and the Christian God*. Grand Rapids, MI: Baker, 1982.

Pinnock, Clark, ed. *The Openness of God: A Biblical Challenge to the Traditional Understanding of God*. Downers Grove, IL: InterVarsity Press, 1994.

Piper, John. *Suffering and the Sovereignty of God*. Wheaton, IL: Crossway Books, 2006.

Plantinga, Alvin. *God, Freedom and Evil*. London: Allen and Unwin, 1974.

———. *The Nature of Necessity*. Oxford: Clarendon Press, 1974.

Rice, Richard. "Biblical Support for a New Position." In Pinnock, *Openness of God*, 11–58.

Rogers, Jack. *Biblical Authority*. Nashville, TN: Word, 1977.

Rogers, Jack, and Donald K. McKim. *The Authority and Interpretation of the Bible: An Historical Approach*. New York: Harper & Row, 1979.

Roth, John K. "A Theology of Protest." In *Encountering Evil: Live Options in Theodicy*, edited by Stephen T. Davis, 7–22. Louisville, KY: Westminster John Knox Press, 2001.

Sanders, Jack T. "Wisdom, Theodicy, Death, and the Evolution of Intellectual Traditions." *Journal for the Study of Judaism in the Persian, Hellenistic and Roman Period* 36, no. 3 (2005): 263–77. ATLA Religion Database.

Schilling, S. Paul. *God and Human Anguish*. Nashville, TN: Abingdon, 1977.

Sittser, Gerald L. *A Grace Disguised: How the Soul Grows Through Loss*. Grand Rapids, MI: Zondervan, 1996.

Smedes, Lewis B. "What's God Up To? A Father Grieves the Loss of a Child." *Christian Century* 120, no. 9 (May 3, 2003): 38–39.

Stackhouse, John Gordon. *Can God Be Trusted? Faith and the Challenge of Evil*. New York: Oxford University Press, 1998.

Surin, Kenneth. *Theology and the Problem of Evil*. Eugene, OR: Wipf & Stock, 1986.

Swinburne, Richard. *Providence and the Problem of Evil.* Oxford: Clarendon Press, 1998.

Tada, Joni Eareckson. *When God Weeps: Why Our Sufferings Matter to the Almighty.* Grand Rapids, MI: Zondervan, 1997.

Tillich, Paul. *Systematic Theology.* Vol 1. Chicago: University of Chicago Press, 1951.

Vieth, Richard F. *Holy Power, Human Pain.* Bloomington, IN: Meyer-Stone Books, 1988.

Weatherhead, Leslie D. *The Will of God.* Nashville, TN: Abingdon, 1972.

Whitney, Barry L. *Evil and the Process God.* New York: E. Mellen Press, 1985.

Wiersbe, Warren W. *Why Us? When Bad Things Happen to God's People.* Old Tappan, NJ: Revell, 1984.

Willimon, William H. *Sighing for Eden: Sin, Evil, and the Christian Faith.* Nashville, TN: Abingdon Press, 1985.

Yancey, Philip. *Disappointment with God: Three Questions No One Asks Aloud.* Grand Rapids, MI: Zondervan, 1988.

―――. *Prayer: Does It Make Any Difference?* Grand Rapids, MI: Zondervan, 2006.

―――. *Where Is God When It Hurts?* Grand Rapids, MI: Zondervan, 1977.

Zurheide, Jeffry. *When Faith Is Tested: Pastoral Responses to Suffering and Tragic Death.* Minneapolis, MN: Fortress Books, 1997.